BACKLASH: SAVING GLOBALISATION
FROM ITSELF

A book for this perilous moment

Trade is politics. So trade policy should follow a country's domestic and foreign policy objectives. Yet, globalisation is draining power from many countries' national polity, through persistent trade imbalances, apparently invulnerable global corporations and dominant trading blocs.

The backlash is already to be seen: China using trade to deliver long-term strategic political gain; President Trump castigating the US trade deficits; populist movements against globalisation.

Joe Zammit-Lucia and David Boyle don't just highlight these conflicts. They challenge a trading system based on twentieth century structures and nineteenth century ideas. They question fundamental assumptions about comparative advantage in the face of rapidly-evolving disruptive technologies and capital flows driven by tax arbitrage. And they offer proposals for reform rightly focusing on competition, innovative enterprise and mutual regulatory convergence.

This is a book for this perilous moment; whether facing up to Brexit, populism or protectionism.

Politicians, who have too often taken the inevitability of globalisation, and with it the benefits of free trade, for granted, need now to read this and think fresh thoughts, radical thoughts, about how to make trade again serve the public and our democracies, not overbear them.

The Rt Hon the Lord Lansley
UK Co-Chairman, UK-Japan 21st Century Group

BACKLASH

Saving globalisation from itself

Joe Zammit-Lucia
David Boyle

www.radix.org.uk

This edition published in 2018 by Radix.
www.radix.org.uk © Radix
A Kindle edition is also available.

The moral right of Joe Zammit-Lucia and David Boyle to be identified as the author of this work has been asserted in accordance with the Copyright, Designs and Patents Acts of 1988.

Print ISBN 9780995609990

Printed by CPI Group (UK) Limited, Croydon CR0 4YY

Acknowledgements

We would like to thank the many who have written and been engaged in the complex task of creating a successful framework for international trade over many decades. This book is based on their work; work that has benefited countless people worldwide and provides useful lessons for the future.

Particular thanks go to Robert McDougall for detailed and highly insightful comments, patient explanations and suggestions on multiple drafts.

We are also grateful to Sir Nick Clegg, Robert Madelin, Miriam González-Durántez, Magdalena Polan, Nick Silver, Nick Tyrone and Simon Zadek for generously agreeing to read early drafts and devoted time to providing extensive comments without which this book would not have happened.

All remaining errors of fact or judgement are entirely the authors' own.

*Dedicated to everyone involved in the successful
launch of the Radix think tank network*

Contents

"I sympathize, therefore, with those who would minimize, rather than with those who would maximize, economic entanglement among nations. Ideas, knowledge, science, hospitality, travel--these are the things which should of their nature be international. But let goods be homespun whenever it is reasonably and conveniently possible, and, above all, let finance be primarily national. Yet, at the same time, those who seek to disembarrass a country of its entanglements should be very slow and wary. It should not be a matter of tearing up roots but of slowly training a plant to grow in a different direction."

John Maynard Keynes, 1933

Foreword

Is globalization a consequence of international trade? Or is it a product of many other factors and international trade is simply one of the ways in which globalization manifests itself? Is international trade policy an instrument of foreign and economic policy? Or, on the contrary, is foreign policy a way for a country to enhance its trade links? Joe Zammit-Lucia and David Boyle aim not only to find an answer to these fundamental questions, but also to make a series of recommendations to 'humanise' trade policy and fix what in their view are some of the flaws of free trade.

Globalisation does not necessarily equate with free trade. Odysseus, the Roman Empire generals, the Portuguese and Spanish conquistadors, the British scientific explorers, the Italian renaissance painters, the Swedish female tourists who in the 60s introduced bikinis in Franco's Spain, the Beatles ... were not traders, but they were all agents of globalization. They built on the inner wish of most individuals to expand beyond their immediate neighbourhood, to emulate what others in other parts of the world do, to rise above their cultural horizons and live in a world without constraints. Even countries whose trade is closed to the outside world cannot isolate their populations from the cultural influences of people elsewhere: nowhere is this more apparent than in Iran, where due to sanctions trade with the rest of the world has been virtually impossible during the last 15 years and yet a large part of its population lives in permanent awe of the 'American way of life'.

It is probably because globalization has been wrongly identified with free trade that blaming free trade for most of the challenges of the modern world has now become the order of the day. And not only for populist politicians, but for mainstream ones as well: protectionist rhetoric is on the up, tariffs are little by little increasing, national security is being used as an excuse for countries to fight foreign bids and 'tit-for-tat' trade retaliation is making a comeback. Just as it is easier for politicians in the West to blame social discontent on 'the others' (the Mexicans, the Arabs, the Europeans...) than on their own policy mistakes, it is also easier for them to blame declining living standards, lack of productivity of their economies, or poor innovation and skills on alleged trade abuses from third countries than on the inadequacy of the policies that they have set up themselves.

And yet, while the blame game against globalization and free trade is starting to leave its political and economic imprint on the world, Joe Zammit-Lucia and David Boyle are right to question whether the current international trade system is fit for the dynamics of our age. In a world defined by the loss of trust (between the East and the West, the developing and the developed world, between populations and the political class, the working class and the elite and between people and technology) is it possible to continue operating with a trade system whose structure is based precisely on cooperation and trust? And more to the point, is the trade system able to cope with the pace of change that runs our world today?

The World Trade Organisation system that governs the rules of trade for last 23 years is indeed based on trust. It is an attempt at cooperation amongst countries, rather than a cold pursuit of their economic interests at the expense of everybody else. Developed countries and regions, especially the powerful ones such as the US and the EU, gave up their ability to impose their trade power on others on the basis of their own sheer economic strength. In exchange they obtained a commitment from most other countries to open up their goods and services markets for the benefit of all: lower tariffs, liberalized services and commitments to reduce technical barriers to trade.

3

Complaints abound that the disciplines of the World Trade Organisation are too rigid. It is indeed difficult for the WTO system, which is based on unanimous decisions from all countries at the same time, to cope with the mutability of the current trade patterns, where foreign investment moves at incredible speed. But the fact is that what has led to the general discontent with the current international trade system is arguably a lack of effective WTO governance, rather than an excess of it.

While the focus of the international trade system has been on market access and equal treatment of foreign companies as national ones, there has been consistent reluctance (not only from developing countries and China but also from developed countries that have traditionally championed free trade) to address the distorting effects of low regulatory standards, especially on intellectual property, taxes, environmental and labour laws. As a result, blue collar workers in developed countries are regularly asked to compete with those from countries where basic labour standards and regulatory thresholds are significantly lower than in their own countries or do not even exist. If a country is forced politically by others to increase those standards, the foreign investment and supply chains simply move elsewhere. In the face of this obvious unfairness, there is little the WTO or even bilateral trade agreements can do in practice to address those concerns.

The challenge for the international trade system is not whether there is a magic recipe of 'just enough free trade': a little bit of openness combined with the right measure of protectionism, that would seamlessly allow countries to profit from lower prices for their consumers and prosper while retaining their well-earned skills and know-how. Such optimal level of free trade does not exist. And if it did, governments would certainly struggle to find it: government intervention has not managed to find an 'optimal' level of trade even when supply chains moved slowly, so it is unlikely they would be able to do so today when trade moves at a much more rapid pace.

Despite the calls of those calling for more protectionism (whether openly or through the back door) the challenge of modern trade is not the level of free trade, but about the conditions attached to such trade. Countries should be able to exploit legitimately their advantages, competitive positions and the differences in the way they address their own economies and work forces as they see fit. However, the abuse of those competitive advantages by lowering standards below basic rights, disregarding environmental threats and disregarding compliance against financial crime, risks leading countries into a downwards regulatory spiral in which nobody can gain. More worryingly, it risks undermining the basic trust of people in the international rule of trade law. It is therefore no wonder that most trade negotiations nowadays, including those on Brexit, focus not just on opening markets, but also on ensuring a 'level playing field'.

Even disregarding Brexit, where the misconceptions about free trade abound, the political narrative around free trade is increasingly being based on impossibly naïve demands: the belief that free trade should 'benefit all' as if anything in the world has ever benefited 'all' without a cost to anybody else; and the dream of some to be able to close down trade borders to regain control without it having any impact on the prosperity of their own countries, or their trading partners, or both. In the long run, however, the fundamentals of free trade are likely to be safe, as free trade runs in the next generation's DNA: a generation that knows no borders, 'made in' labels or even basic awareness about the complex logistics behind the products that they consume.

But while all these wider philosophical debates develop and take place, the real question is a much simpler one: do we have the will and the tools to make free trade fairer trade? Because nobody, whether in developing or developed countries, should be put in the position of having to compete with unfair trade.

Miriam González-Durántez
International and EU trade lawyer
Co-Chair International and EU Trade Practice,
Dechert LLP

1

Trade, prosperity and suffering

"The old is dying and the new cannot be born; in this interregnum, a great variety of morbid symptoms appear"

Antonio Gramsci

G o to Nathan Road in Kowloon, part of Hong Kong, and you will find Chungking Mansions. From the outside, it looks like so many other blocks built in the early 1960s, but from the inside, it is very different. Once a residential block for ethnic Chinese people, it now provides homes and inexpensive business accommodation for more than 4,000 people from all over the world. Not for the rich, but for traders and small entrepreneurs from every corner of the globe.

It has garnered a great deal of journalistic attention, partly because it is so rare – a corner of multi-ethnic enterprise on a tiny scale. Time magazine has even called it the best "example of globalisation in action" in the world.[1] But its rarity is interesting in itself. Because, in so many other trading city states – indeed, in most of the rest of Hong Kong – the pattern of globalisation has driven out this kind of small-scale entrepreneurial energy. It has driven up property prices to price out most people.

There are people who might say that Chungking Mansions represents the real thing. It is in that sense a kind of globalisation for everyone, for the average business, compared to the slick, finance driven towers of globalisation for the wealthy alone. This great division – symbolised by this unusual mansion block – between one form of globalisation and another – lies behind so many of the intractable issues of our time. It also lies behind this book.

Trade and prosperity

There is nothing new about international trade.

In 3000 BC the people of Mesopotamia were trading with the people of the Indus Valley in what is today Pakistan. Soon thereafter the idea of self-sufficiency, that you had to produce yourself everything that you needed or wanted, started to fade. Trade networks spread across Eurasia. Cultures and economies became linked for the first time. The domestication of camels in 1000 BC made land-based trade a viable alternative to more expensive sea routes. India became linked to the Mediterranean. New towns and cities sprang up along trading routes - land routes, sea ports and rivers.

Trade was the route to prosperity for many. China prospered by selling its jade, spices and silks;

Phoenicia its cedar woods and linen dyes; Britain its tin. Just like today, middlemen prospered most of all.

As economies became more complex and trading increased, so trading also became more complex and multifaceted. From the fifteenth to the eighteenth centuries, international trade morphed into mercantilism – the belief that a country could only prosper if it had a positive trade balance with other countries and thereby accumulate monetary reserves. Tariffs and other anti-trade measures grew as countries sought to maintain the upper hand as trade morphed from a general convenience to competition between nations.

Further liberalisation came in the eighteenth and nineteenth centuries following the ideas of Adam Smith and David Ricardo. The idea of comparative advantage suggested that countries should only focus on doing that which they are good at – that which they can produce at lower opportunity cost – and trade with others for the remaining goods. This was the start of what today we might call de-industrialisation.

Countries would start to shed skills and production and give up markets to countries that were considered to have a comparative advantage. For many countries, the net result was a loss of skills built up over centuries and which could not easily be re-built as the nature of supposed comparative advantage between nations changed over time. For some, including the UK, the long-term effect was hugely damaging.

Soon enough the fundamental problem was no longer the ability to trade. A new monster had been born, and it was called monopoly power. Once again, international trade provided one part of the solution. In 1846 Peel, following Cobden, joined the Whigs and the Radicals to repeal the Corn Laws in

Trade policy oscillates between openness and withdrawal

an assault on the monopoly power of the land-owning aristocracy that wanted to keep food prices high and supply limited even in the face of people dying of famine. It was a vindication of Adam Smith's original warning that collusion between entrenched interests ends in *"a conspiracy against the public"*.

The new free trade was designed as a means of liberation from the Frankenstein born to the free trade system that had gone before – monopoly power. The clear objective of the new trade liberalisation was to make sure that the small could challenge the big, the poor could challenge the rich with the power of the new approach, the alternative provider, the imaginative, liberating shift.

Trade has since oscillated constantly between openness and withdrawal, with nobody being comfortable for long with either. The early twentieth century showed further moves towards liberalisation. The First World War changed that course with countries building barriers to trade. Post-war liberalisation was short lived. The Great Depression of the 1920s saw a return to tariffs and other barriers.

The complexity of modern economies also meant that trade agreements became increasingly convoluted. There was also a desire to create a framework through which the larger and more powerful nations would not always be in a position to subjugate the weaker ones – the nation-level equivalent of monopoly power.

Multilateral Trade Agreements were born. The General Agreement on Tariffs and Trade in 1947 laid the ground for the trade system that we have today and the evolution from nation-level agreements to today's multi-lateral agreements within and between trading blocks.

So what?

There are important lessons to be learnt from even such a cursory glance at the history of international trade. Lessons we would do well to take to heart today.

> Like natural systems, international trade is a delicate dance between collaboration and competition

The first is that international trade is, and always has been, a dance between competition and co-operation – much like we see in complex adaptive natural systems. It's a delicate dance and the steps change as the music changes over time. Trade has never been an end in itself. It should be considered a tool of foreign and domestic policy. The over-riding questions for any government should be: how does international trade effect the social, political and economic structures of our country; and how does trade, and the shape of our trade agreements, fit with our foreign policy goals.

> **Trade is a tool for governments' domestic and foreign policy goals not an end in itself**

The second is that the structure and approach to trade has never been stable. It has always oscillated and changed depending on the political and economic conditions of the day. Countries grew *"familiar to the fact that the old schools of thought were no longer going to be practical and that they had to keep reviewing their international trade policies on continuous basis."* We believe that we are currently in the midst of another of these great changes.

Finally, trade has always brought both benefits and disadvantages. Over time, trade structures resulted in prosperity for some and suffering for others. Those who accumulated advantages became ever wealthier and more powerful. Eventually their power had to be broken by firm and decisive intervention.

We desperately need the next great transition

We are entering an era of great danger to world peace and harmony. The post-war international order led by the US started breaking down following the atrocity of 9/11. Polarisation is now the order of the day. We are approaching a situation where every nation or bloc fights for its own self-interest in a beggar-thy-neighbour approach.[2]

The backlash against globalisation and international trade can be considered both a symptom of this dangerous trend and a partial cause, seeing as the adverse effects of globalisation are themselves

> **We are entering an era of great danger to world peace and harmony**

contributing factors driving the polarisation. All this has made globalisation among the main political, economic and social issues of our time.

Rather than just bemoaning these developments, wishing them away and insisting that things must stay as they are, we must act. It is imperative, therefore, that we have the courage to ask fundamental questions. What does globalisation really mean? Is it a good thing or a bad thing? Or a bit of both? Has it been the fountain of prosperity for billions? Is it one of the underpinnings of rising inequality? Is the current free trade structure appropriate for today's geopolitical landscape? Should we start sounding the retreat from a supposedly 'globalised world'? Or is that a sure road to rack and ruin? If we are to preserve a harmonious and peaceful world, is it time to revisit the foundations on which our current conception of globalisation is built?

In a complex world, most of what is going on is the result of the interaction of many moving parts. It would not be wise to draw simple and direct cause and effect relationships. But there is now little doubt that the way that globalisation has evolved is a significant contributing factor to the discontent and the polarisation. As we shall clearly show in this book, it is time to get beyond what has become the banal mantra that 'free trade is a net benefit and must be preserved' – a statement that has, for some, become an excuse for idle inaction even as the whole edifice is threatened with collapse.

> **The current shape of globalisation is fueling significant discontent and political instability**

Refusing to countenance any flaws that have arisen as a result of the current international trade model; or to consider that what might have served us well in the past might be ripe for revamping, simply fuels the anger and rhetoric of those for whom open trade lies at the root of most evils. For them, the system must be torn down and walls – real and metaphorical – must be constructed.

This book takes a different tack. We reject the 'either/or' formulation of the issues. Free trade has brought benefit to many. AND, in its current form, it has evolved substantial flaws. They need fixing.

We reject the framing of the issue as one of ideology – a false dichotomy between maintaining the current trading system as is or face a breakdown of any sort of rules-based international order. It is plain wrong to characterise the moment as one where nations have to "choose which ideology to rally behind."[3] This is not, and cannot be made to be, about ideology. It is about the practicalities of making international trade work in a world that has changed and where previous assumptions no longer hold.

We also believe that those individuals and institutions that have influence over the shape and nature of international trade have a moral duty to act. In these fragile geopolitical times, standing

It is time to ensure that international trade can continue to deliver widespread and visible benefits

idly by and pointing the finger elsewhere is simply irresponsible.

Times have changed. The needs of twenty-first century economies are different from what they were in the past. The nature and shape of the geopolitical landscape has been transformed.

We therefore believe that it is time to have a broad debate on the free trade framework so that it can be improved and continues to deliver more benefits than disadvantages. That such benefits are widely visible to the general population. And that the international trade framework is appropriate to meet most government's foreign and domestic policy goals – something that may be becoming more difficult to achieve.

We believe that, as is inevitable with any long-running framework, the free trade agenda has become progressively captured by powerful interests; those who have focused on developing the skills to take advantage of a complexity that others cannot easily navigate. As a result, the system ends up serving such powerful interests disproportionately, to the detriment of the objectives which open trade was meant to achieve.

We are at risk of transitioning from democracy to plutocracy

The issues associated with our current trade framework are a result of failure to tackle them adequately over the last half-century. Since 1846, we have not had another Cobden moment. On the contrary, vested interests have continued to accumulate power and democratically elected national governments have progressively become ever more emasculated. To an extent that we are now at real risk of transitioning seamlessly from democracy to plutocracy.

Rather than being able and willing to protect against Adam Smith's conspiracies against the public, governments and multilateral institutions seem to have been in thrall to, and subjugated by, entrenched interests. Interests that have managed to convince many that their own perspective is the only route to general prosperity.

People have started to feel all this in their bones. They see its effect in their everyday lives. This has fueled the rise of what some choose to call 'populist' political forces. Forces that call for the re-assertion of the sovereignty of national, democratically elected Governments and the protection of local communities and local cultures against what they see as the ravages of globalisation and excessive openness.

While it may be true that such forces offer what may be simplistic solutions to complex issues, the grievances on which they feed are real, not imagined. In refusing to acknowledge these grievances, resisting change, and being unwilling or unable to offer their own solutions, mainstream political groups become the essential fuel behind the continued rise of reactionary forces.

The greater the resistance to change, the more destructive will be the reaction to the status quo. As regards international trade, it is time for the next great transition – as in the many transitions we have seen over the ages. Such a transition must first and foremost keep in mind the original purpose of free trade - not as an end in itself but merely as a means to an end. That end being increased harmony, prosperity and social cohesion for all. If that is either forgotten or allowed to be marginalized by narrow but powerful interests, then the backlash against free trade will continue to rise.

Eventually, it will become destructive while those 'in charge' look on with dismay, unable to comprehend how people can possibly contemplate such destructive action.

It is may be one of the great paradoxes – stability can only come from embracing change. Change that visibly adapts to the times.

Stability only comes from embracing change

Also, the current format of trade agreements risks achieving very little. The EU-Canada trade deal took five years to negotiate, achieved little liberalisation in services and a very weak form of regulatory convergence. It was very nearly de-railed by the opposition of the Walloon government in Belgium. The complexity of the current trade system means that agreements have become narrow and shallow.[4] It seems like being able to showcase a new trade agreement has become a political end in itself irrespective of whether the results are meaningful or not.

The questions we address in this book are these:

- Are the fundamental assumptions on which the free trade system has been built still relevant in a 21st century world?

- If free trade underpinning globalisation is one of the factors behind the discontent at the heart of the global political crisis, might there be another and more effective way of doing free trade – so that the rewards are more widespread and more visible to all?

- Given the nature of a twenty-first century political economy, what are the appropriate next steps in the evolution of our approach to international trade?

We also hope that, in a world where globalisation has become one of the more contentious political and social issues of our time, this book might offer those not embedded in the subject an accessible overview of the issues involved.

This book is divided into three sections.

In the first section we examine the changing global context. We examine how both social attitudes and the structure of the world economy have changed and we question how many of the original tenets on which our current free trade system is based still hold.

We put forward ideas for new approaches that could start to recapture the original spirit of free trade and ensure that it continues to be effective for all in a twenty-first century world.

In the second section, we examine what the Brexit phenomenon tells us about people's appetite for what globalisation seems to have become. We also examine what today's context of free trade might mean for potential post-Brexit trade deals. The long-term consequences of Brexit are largely unknown. Yet the fact of Brexit itself must surely teach us something. We need to ensure that we do not learn the wrong lessons.

It is human to under-play the adverse effects of our well-intentioned actions

Finally, we bring together some overall conclusions.

It is human to under-play the adverse effects of our well-intentioned actions. But if we are to improve and make things better, we need to face these issues without minimising the achievements. That purpose underpins this book.

I

Globalisation: Towards a New Settlement

2

Globalisation in reverse

*"I have often reflected that the
causes of the successes or failures
or men depend upon their manner
of suiting their conduct to the
times."*

Niccolo Machiavelli

The mere idea of trade deals has confused the usual dividing lines of mainstream politics. Normally, the radical Left is dismissive of free trade as making the world safe for plutocracy, while the Right believes the free market is a conservative institution that stabilises the world.

Recent events have reversed those positions. The Right is now suspicious of free trade, internationalism and immigration, while the Left clings on to the idea of free trade they have criticised for so long. Neither the old-fashioned Right nor the old-fashioned Left seem to grasp, let alone accept, that trade deals, as a basis for freer trade, require some loss of sovereignty.

Both sides are right in this case, but some naivety lies behind it. Trade deals are complex exhausting animals which tend to over-reach themselves by straying into areas that are not necessary for freer trade.

But something is stirring out there. The centre ground of politics has taken a battering, but the remaining idea that binds it together has always been a basic right to do business across borders and with anyone that people see fit to buy from and sell to. Traditionally, that right underpinned so many other freedoms too.

> The right to do business across borders has always underpinned the political centre ground

The new 21ˢᵗ century language

In a few short years, 'globalisation' has been transformed in public discourse from a symbol of hip prosperity to being synonymous with unfairness, inequality and plutocracy. Both positions overstate their case. But what we cannot ignore is that, while people will always continue to trade with each other as much as they can, the idea of unfettered hyper-globalisation has, for the moment, run its course.

A new global order is emerging because, while not denying the success of open trade to date, the status quo is now widely seen as being unsustainable. Yet we remain short of ideas about how to respond. How to reform the framework of global trade to maintain the benefits while reversing the adverse effects.

In this chapter, we go through the basis on which transnational trade was built. We explore how many of the assumptions and mainstream thinking underlying international trade have evolved and changed. These changes can be broken down into three main categories: political, cultural and economic.

The table below puts forward some suggested comparisons between the characteristics of the late twentieth century, post-war global order and the emergent 21st century one. We then address some of these key changes in some more detail.

Late twentieth Century Global Order	Early twenty-first Century Emergent Features
1. Political	
Global free trade overseen by global governance structures. Individual countries sacrificing sovereignty for economic growth opportunities	Rise of forces that re-assert the nation state as the primary locus of democratic legitimacy. Politics' primary responsibility is to its own citizens

Politics of prosperity through the free flow of finance, goods and services	Reaction against the threat to democratic legitimacy by trans-national economic forces at the expense of citizens and their governments through arbitrage between countries in investment, jobs and taxes
Western political hegemony with liberal democracy as aspirational goal for all countries	Multiple centres of power. Liberal democracy only one of many alternative political structures. Multiple failures to replace autocratic regimes with democratic structures
Trade between large number of smaller economic players (plus a single hegemon – the US) supported a rules-based, cooperative multilateral system under US leadership	Trade agenda dominated by three major trading blocs more likely to lead to competitive rather than co-operative behaviour
National security seen as largely separate from trade	National security issues become enmeshed with trade practices

2. Cultural

Free movement of people and 'multi-culturalism'	Social cohesion fundamental to sustaining functioning societies and social solidarity
Cultural and religious co-existence	Culture wars and identity politics
Increase in global communication opens up global markets and mutual exchange	Concern over concentrated control of communications platforms, potential abuse of personal data, fake news, and cultural, political and national security impact of uncontrolled social media platforms
Consumption is king and perpetual growth the aim	Concerns on the sustainability of consumption-driven growth in a world of finite resources

3. Economic

Comparative advantage underpins global trade	Comparative advantage no longer sustainable
'Mercantilism' a dirty word	Increased concern about the impact of perpetual trade deficits
Global value chains bring down costs and increase prosperity	Local production increasingly valued. Closed Loop value chains emerging
Externalities largely ignored	Environmental and social costs of globalisation becoming more difficult to ignore

The New World Order

Recognising the move towards a more interconnected world, the post-war global elite envisioned a new world order. Countries would co-operate to devise a system of 'global governance' where a set of clear rules would be agreed upon, everyone would abide by them and stability and certainty would reign. International institutions – the League of Nations (later the UN), the IMF, the World Bank, NATO, Bretton Woods, the European

Economic Community (later the EU) – were the poster children of the new world order.

In this new world, globalisation and ever-growing international trade would be a positive. It would interlink economies, diminish the chances of conflict and spread prosperity around the globe. The international elite would be in charge and would steer the whole globe to peace and prosperity.

This system worked well for decades. It is starting to fray at the edges. And for many reasons.

The structure of free trade deals is driven by the relative power of the players involved. Each party will fight for a structure that suits its own national interest. Relative power is largely a function of the size of the respective economies and their growth prospects.

The late twentieth century was characterised by US hegemony and multiple smaller players whose self-interest lay in cooperation and multilateralism – albeit all steered by the US and its dominant framing and support of the post-war world order. The twenty-first century, on the other hand, is characterized by the dominance of three more-or-less equally powerful trading blocs: the US, the EU and China with its growing sphere of influence.

It is not yet clear where Russia will end up in this new alignment. Whether it will attempt to strike out on its own and create yet another bloc of influence.

In a world dominated by three trading blocs, competition rather than cooperation will drive world trade

Or whether it will slowly align with one of the existing blocs. To put it another way, will any of the three main blocs manage to win over for themselves Russia and its sphere of influence?

The potential impact of the three-bloc world has long been clear. In a 1989 paper, Paul Krugman constructed a model that concluded that:[5]

> *"Consolidation of the world into a smaller number of trading blocs may indeed reduce welfare, even when each bloc acts to maximize the welfare of its members. Indeed, for all plausible parameter values world welfare is minimized when there are three trading blocs."*

This is exactly what is emerging. Global trade today is framed by competition between large trading blocs with the attendant risk that multilateralism will collapse and countries that are outside of these trading blocs will find themselves at permanent disadvantage.

The rise of China has served to highlight these issues for Western powers. According to the Economist:

> "[The West] bet that China would head towards democracy and the market economy. The gamble has failed."[6]

That gamble has failed politically. But it has also failed in terms of the hopes for integrating China into a Western-led international trading system. It can reasonably be argued that China has proceeded down what we might call 'Free trade with Chinese characteristics'. *"China is not a market economy and, on its present course, never will be. Instead, it increasingly controls business as an arm of state power."*[6]

China initially gained its power by being seen as providing the best source of future growth for Western business. Now it forms one of the three trading blocs and is able to gain advantageous terms of trade. It showed itself able to work the system to its advantage. China uses its leverage to force foreign companies to transfer skills and technology to local companies as the price for access to the Chinese market.

China practices what one might call free trade with Chinese characteristics

> *"In industries from power generation to high-speed rail and computer chips to electric cars, China has forced US, European and other*

33

foreign companies to form joint ventures or share research with local counterparts. Access to China's booming marketplace is often linked explicitly or implicitly to the foreign company's progress in transferring technology."[7]

This approach has been described as 'unfair and sometimes cynical' but it has worked – because China learned to use its power to extract concessions from its trading partners. Since its accession to the WTO, China has, if anything, doubled down on its approach. Its 'Made in China 2025' plan unveiled in 2015 calls for widespread import substitution by domestic products and the favouring of national companies at the expense of multinationals.

"No wonder the greatest beneficiaries of globalisation were nations like China that eschewed the official rules and danced to the beat of their own drum. It and other Asian countries engaged the world economy but did so on their own terms: they employed trade and industrial policies prohibited by the World Trade Organisation, managed their currencies, and kept tight controls on international capital flows."[8]

China's approach has generated suspicion and defensiveness. Dr Kai-Fu Lee, Chairman and CEO of Sinovation Ventures, put it like this during a recent visit to the UK:

"If the UK is to keep its position as a leading research hub for AI it will need increasingly

to build bridges with counterparts in China.
The number of hyper-engaged users and vast
oceans of data mean that the market is ripe to
harness the cutting-edge research happening
in the UK."⁹

Today, many people reading these words are, rightly or wrongly, tempted to interpret 'building bridges' as code for the transfer of technology, know-how and intellectual property in return for limited market access that will only be allowed in close collaboration with local partners and with the ever-present long arm of the state.

Neither, argue some, is protectionism an issue limited to China. Many have accused the EU of protectionist tendencies through the erection of regulatory barriers - an issue we shall come to again later.

China can, of course, argue that its approach is perfectly reasonable. It cannot maintain an economy that is successful in the long term by permanently remaining the low-cost workshop of the world. It therefore has to manage its trade policies to make

China refuses to swallow, hook, line and sinker, the fable of neo-liberal economics

sure that it grows skills, capabilities and industries that are going to be internationally competitive in the future. Who can argue against that?

Maybe what distinguishes China above all else is that it has refused to swallow, hook, line and sinker, the fable spun by neo-liberal economics.

The open free trade system we know today was initially driven by the West (particularly the UK at the height of its imperial and industrial power, and subsequently by the US). It is largely a Western construct. At its peak, and driven by its colonial success, the West was dominant and more technologically advanced than other countries. An open trading system therefore served it well. It was able to dominate markets. It could reasonably be argued that the system was not 'fair'. It simply favoured those in charge.

Yet the West either failed to recognise or simply failed to accept the finite nature of dominance.

Trump is right: Free trade with Western characteristics may no longer serve most of the Western world well

Maybe with typical short-termism, there was no adequate preparation for a changing world. The West is now reaping the consequences. The reality is that while an open trading system that it largely controlled served Western interests in the past, it may no longer do so to the same extent today. The same can be said of all other countries as the nature of comparative advantage changes (see next section).

In challenging the established order of international trade, Donald Trump may well have intuited something that seems to have passed his predecessors and his opponents by – in the new multi-polar world, the old system may no longer be serving America well.

China's approach seems to be more forward looking. It is using the position it finds itself in today to build for a future it knows will be different. Its Belt and Road initiative creates a large, Chinese-funded sphere of influence that, crucially, asks countries to sign up to dispute resolution mechanisms that are under Chinese control.

Loss of trust

In such a world, it is unsurprising that there has been a widespread loss of trust between countries and blocs. And post-war global governance institutions are no longer seen as either legitimate or effective.

Many emerging economies feel that they do not have a sufficient voice in global governance institutions that *"have had trouble adapting to the rise of the emerging economies: the United States and Europe still dominate them, eroding their credibility and influence among developing countries, especially in Asia."*[10]

Western countries, on the other hand, have started to feel that such institutions, besides being neither democratically legitimate nor properly accountable, can no longer serve their interests in a changing world. Yes, the West continues to dominate these institutions, but that is insufficient to stem the tide of power flowing from West to East.

In short, we may be headed to a new Hobbesian world where competition trumps co-operation. And where there has been a significant loss of trust – both in the system itself and in the arbitrators of that system. Some argue that *"With cooperation unlikely, the world should prepare itself for erosion of the World Trade Organisation."*[11]

Free trade, sovereignty and democracy

It has finally dawned on many that free trade involves some loss of sovereignty for nation states. Pooling of decision-making across countries is inevitable if trade is to flow. Free trade agreements *"reach well beyond national borders and seek deep integration among nations rather than shallow integration."*[12]Harvard professor Dani Rodrik argues that democracy, globalisation and the sovereignty of nation states are mutually incompatible.[13] We can imagine them as three rings held together by elastic bands. The more one

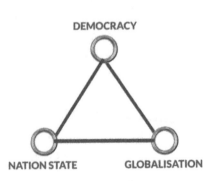

DEMOCRACY

NATION STATE   GLOBALISATION

pulls on one or the other, the more the others have to give. Rodrik argues that globalisation may have gone too far at the expense of democratic accountability that rests primarily with the nation state.

This was not an issue in the post-war world. Then the focus was on a US led economic recovery from the devastation of war and the desire to use trade to bind nations together and prevent further conflict. The fact that the huge rise in international trade at the turn of the previous century had failed to prevent the First World War seems to have been forgotten. Yet, the post-war international trade structure was aligned with the prevailing foreign policy environment where, except for the Soviet Union, by and large, co-operation was preferred to confrontation, and all was done under the umbrella of US leadership.

Post-1945, sovereignty and national and cultural identity were not top of people's minds. In a globalising world, national and sub-national identities were considered a hindrance to progress and, more locally, identity was equated with class wars, religious intolerance, ghettoisation and all manner of other evils. The powerful nation state was seen by some as the enemy of peace.

Progress was to turn us all into rational global citizens, looking beyond the parochial to the global. In other words, the richness of culture, history and specific identities were all to be subordinated to the common global (largely American) culture. We were all to change from citizens with complex, deeply rooted local identities to citizens of the world in order to benefit from globalisation.

Sovereignty, meanwhile, would be shared or pooled – even though nobody quite knew how this was to be successfully achieved. Neither did anyone bother to seek popular consent. It was an elite decision that was believed to be for the greater good.

The end of the cold war further embedded Western complacency and, some would say, hubris. The much heralded 'peace dividend' was largely frittered away. The West had won the battle of ideas. It was the end of history. An economically integrated, globalized world based on the inevitable spread of liberal democratic values would seal the dominance of Western ideals and Western economic hegemony.

> There is a palpable backlash against the loss of sovereignty, local culture and local identity that has resulted from globalisation

We could now afford to de-militarise much like we had already de-industrialised. The new cultural colonialism was to be spearheaded by the relentless spread of MacDonald's outlets and Starbucks coffee.

All this has changed. The backlash against the perceived erosion of local culture and identity as a consequence of globalisation has been one of the drivers of a re-emergence of the nation state as the locus of perceived democratic legitimacy. Combined with the increased realisation that trade involves, to a greater or lesser degree, a loss of sovereignty and an erosion of democratic accountability, the current pull is back towards a greater prioritisation of national over supra-national and trans-national interests.

A Europe recovering from the ravages of war pushed post-war thinking further than most. *"The countries of Western Europe must turn their national efforts into a truly European effort. This will be possible only through a federation of the West."*[14] That was Jean Monnet's thinking at the time.

On that road, the European Coal and Steel Community eventually evolved into today's European Union and the Single European Market – a construct where, today, harmonisation has been pushed to levels that are, in some cases, greater than those seen, for instance, between the provinces in Canada or different states in the US. And where, in Europe, the cradle of democracy, the euphemistically named 'democratic deficit' was accepted by the ruling class as the price to be paid for greater integration.

The backlash described above has not passed Europe by. Brexit and the growing rebellions against 'Brussels rule' in a number of other EU countries is causing destabilisation.

The shaky foundations of comparative advantage

*"The principle of comparative advantage
and the case for the gains from trade are
crown jewels of the economics profession."*[15]

The whole edifice of free trade is built on David Ricardo's theory of comparative advantage developed in 1817. Yes, you read correctly, 1817. It holds that a country has comparative advantage in the production of any particular good of equivalent quality when its marginal cost of production is lower than that of other countries.

The theory focuses on the opportunity cost of production rather than the monetary or resource costs. 'Welfare' is maximised when countries focus their production in areas where they had comparative advantage and traded with others where others had comparative advantage. Overall production and consumption would be greater than if each country tried to be self-sufficient in all goods.

The theory was very powerful – in the early nineteenth century. And it underpins everything to do with the global structure of free trade and its economic justification.

But we are now approaching the middle of the twenty-first century. The world has changed beyond all recognition. Yet the theory of comparative advantage still reigns supreme.

There is, of course, nothing to criticise in the theory itself. But much to question about the degree to which it remains applicable in today's and tomorrow's world.

In Ricardo's time, comparative advantage between nations changed only very slowly. The nature of the production of wine and cloth did not change dramatically in a few short years. The transfer of technology and know-how did not happen in

> **The world has changed beyond recognition since the days of David Ricardo**

months. There were not as many multiple definitions of 'quality' as there are today. There were none of the highly sophisticated marketing machines of today's corporations that could magic up new definitions of quality and desirability from essentially similar goods.

So, Ricardo's underlying constraint of goods of equivalent quality largely held true. And, of course, it was a world that traded largely in goods not services.

It is, of course, not for us to embark on a detailed analysis of how much the theory of comparative advantage remains applicable today. There are many who are so much more qualified than we are to do so. But what is astounding is the extent to which a theory that is two centuries old is treated like some indisputable, unarguable and incontestable religious dogma in a world that has changed beyond recognition.

> **Is our free trade structure built on foundations that were once solid and are now turning to quicksand?**

It is astonishing how little debate there is in the public realm about the extent to which it remains applicable in today's world. Those who dare question it are treated as heretics who deserve to be burned at the stake by economists who have been indoctrinated for generations and built their careers on that foundation.

It is time for a serious debate about the degree to which Ricardo's theory remains applicable to today's world. There will be much resistance. Because the implications for the very basis on which our whole trade structure is built risks being profound.

What about equity?

Two things are now widely accepted about the effects of free trade as practiced with a twentieth century mentality based on nineteenth century economics. The first is that trade has increased the size of the economic pie. The second is that those gains have been unevenly spread.

A recent analysis by Christoph Lakner and Branko Milanovic for the World Bank[16] examined the evolution of global interpersonal income inequality between 1988 and 2008. *"In many respects, this might have been the most globalized period ever in history"* according to the authors.

They conclude that, in terms of reducing inequality, 90 per cent of the gains accrued to Asian economies with China the biggest beneficiary of free trade.

> Most of the benefits of trade have accrued to Asian economies and to the wealthiest 1% globally

On the other hand, *"almost 90% of the worst performers are from mature economies."* The other winners have been *'the global one per cent'*.

The chart below shows the net effect. Inequality between nations has decreased while inequality within nations has tended to increase.

In short, the gains from free trade have been asymmetric. The prosperity of the average citizen in the developed world has regressed relative to his or her counterpart in some of the emerging economies and, particularly, relative to the top one per cent of earners in his or her own country.

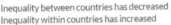

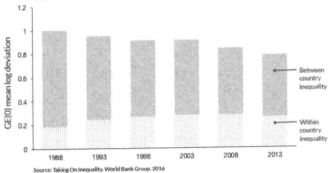

Source: Taking On Inequality. World Bank Group. 2016

Lakner and Milanovic also constructed the now infamous Elephant Chart (figure below). It shows that, over the period examined, the poor and the upper middle classes have been the greatest relative losers in terms of income growth.

According to the IMF, World Bank and WTO,[17]

> *"Adjustment to trade can bring a human and economic downside that is frequently concentrated, sometimes harsh, and has too often become prolonged."*

...as so many people who have been displaced and whose employment prospects have disappeared as a direct result of globalisation have known for many decades before the global governance institutions finally got around to acknowledging the problem.

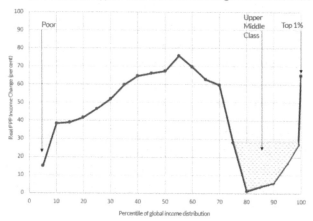

The Poor and the Upper Middle Class have been the greatest relative losers

Of course, increased international trade is not the only thing that has been going on during the period examined by Lakner and Milanovic. We have seen the collapse of the Soviet Union, the rise of China (mainly on the back of trade), and widely variable domestic policy choices in different countries. It is therefore unreasonable to draw a straight-line cause and effect relationship between free trade and the evolution of the spread of income and wealth.

A report by Adam Corlett for the Resolution Foundation[18] deconstructs the Elephant Chart and re-analyses some of the underlying data. Corlett shows that globally aggregated data over long periods inevitably hides wide variations between countries as well as uneven shifts in population and changing country selections over time. The report suggests that:

47

"While global trends are likely to have played a structural role in driving lower income growth for some groups and higher growth for others, it is clearly only one factor among many and the distribution of gains is susceptible to domestic policy choices as much as global pressures."

Such distributional asymmetries were, in fact, predicted by the Stolper-Samuelson model as far back as 1941. In the 1990s many economists assessed these impacts using the Stolper-Samuelson and other models. The general conclusion was that trade would have a wage depressing effect on less educated workers in developed countries. But, at the time, these effects were modest. What economists failed to do was to project the size of that effect if trade were to explode – as it did in the 1990s and beyond. Because the analyses were based on empirical data, and therefore by necessity backward-looking, they lulled everyone into a false sense of security. The major disruptive effects were yet to materialize and were not visible by looking in the rear-view mirror.

Policy cannot be formulated solely by looking in the rear-view mirror

What to do about it

Which brings us to the question of 'domestic policy choices'.

As the IMF, the World Bank and the WTO point out, technology replacement of jobs has been a significant contributor to the dislocations and asymmetric gains that we are seeing. They argue for domestic policies that compensate those considered 'losers' via re-distribution through the social security system as well as better preparation for the dislocations caused by the open trading system.

But, it's not as though countries have been idle in their domestic policies. The figure below shows the impact of re-distribution policies on the Gini Coefficient (so far considered the best measure of inequality) in a number of countries. We can see that governments have been active and redistributive policies have already had a meaningful impact. But it is not enough.

Apart from re-distribution, re-training and lifelong training programmes to make workers more flexible and continually employable as the nature of work changes should also be an integral part of any country's system in a fast-moving world of work. This does not come as news to anyone. But there is scant evidence that such programmes can, in practice, be effective on any significant scale – especially in larger economies. The rust belts of previously industrialised economies still remain, by and large, economic deserts.

Inequality of incomes before and after redistribution

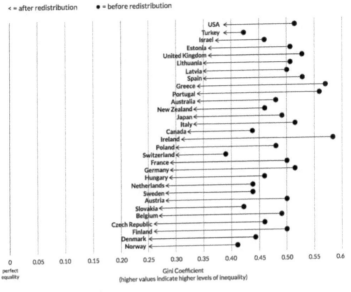

< = after redistribution   ● = before redistribution

0
perfect
equality

Gini Coefficient
(higher values indicate higher levels of inequality)

Data source: OECD
Visualisation adapted from ourworldindata.org

"Such programmes are always likely to be too small to have much effect. They are conceptually very difficult to design, let alone implement; and far from contributing to the political acceptance of globalisation, they may well simply perpetuate an unduly pessimistic view of its effects."[19]

It is also somewhat ironic that the institutional bastions of neo-liberal economics are now arguing for increased government involvement through re-distribution and other government financed support programmes. But in the globalised world under the current rules, this risks simply becoming a downward spiral.

As governments increase their intervention through fiscal means, corporations and capital flee to lower tax jurisdictions, tax arbitrage increases, the bond markets demand higher yields on government debt, government coffers are increasingly squeezed, and on it goes.

Safety nets are necessary, but they may be neither a viable nor a desirable

> **The circle of Right-Left politics: Unfettered free markets eventually lead to greater calls for re-distribution**

long-term solution. People want the dignity and satisfaction offered by decent and decently paid work. Very few relish being converted to wards of the state. The proposed combination of unfettered globalisation, with its now undoubted distributional consequences, and compensatory domestic policies may well be illusory.

We may all point to the few exceptions, such as Denmark, that have managed to find a better balance than others. But it would be hopeful to say the least, if we all simply pinned our hopes for adjustment on the idea that much of the world can successfully imitate the Danish model.

What is quite remarkable is that, still today, many still mechanically trot out the same old line that trade produces a net benefit. It's as though in the world of mathematical economics dissociated from the social and political realities of life, as long as the final single number is positive, it doesn't much matter what else is happening around it. Even today, as

When are the gains from trade worth the distributional, social and political costs?

various bodies calculate the potential impact Trump-driven increase in tariffs, we are regaled with net impact on trade and GDP with the distributional impact only referred to in ideologically laden assertions that anything that interferes with trade must be all bad rather than serious analysis of alternative options.

Even accepting without question that there is a net benefit, nobody seems to ask the question - is the net benefit positive enough to justify the disruption? In other words, are we paying too high a social and political price for the amount of net increase in economic activity (it is plain wrong to keep calling it 'welfare') that accrues from free trade.

Maybe the best answer to that question has been provided in analyses of the impact of NAFTA in the United States.

A multi-sector, multi-country analysis concludes that NAFTA increased US "welfare" by 0.08 percent.[20] BUT – half of this gain did not come from an increase in efficiency but from the US being able to use its muscle to improve its terms of trade (achieved at the expense of other countries, mainly Mexico).

Analysis of the distributional impacts of NAFTA, shows very sharp adverse effects for certain groups of workers. For instance, high school drop-outs working in industries that were heavily protected by tariffs on Mexican exports prior to NAFTA experienced a fall in wage growth of as much as 17 percentage points relative to wage growth in unaffected industries.[21]

Are US gains from NAFTA of less than a tenth of one percent worth the social and political turmoil generated?

So now it's worth asking some questions. Is a gain of less than a tenth of one percent in economic activity worth the social displacements? Has it been a sufficient gain to make us comfortable with the now obvious political consequences of these social disruptions? If we continue down this path what further social and political consequences may we fuel?

President Trump is wrong if he really believes (which is doubtful) that the solution to all this can be found simply in flexing muscle and either negotiating better terms of trade with his partners or slapping tariffs on imports. The whole edifice needs careful re-thinking. Maybe US rhetoric that credibly threatens to bring the whole system down is what is needed to force such a re-think.

Does it take a credible US threat to bring down the whole trading system to force a re-think in how global trade is structured?

That globalisation has a *"structural role in driving lower income growth for some groups and higher growth for others"*, to use Corlett's words, is now beyond dispute. If we are to work towards better outcomes, it is time that we moved past the Punch and Judy show where the opponents of globalisation blame trade as the source of all evil and refuse to do the hard work to reform; while the proponents of international trade sit back and, with an attitude of unchallengeable superiority, try to shift all the burden for adjustment on to domestic policy. International trade policy and domestic policy both need to evolve. And they need to do so in tandem, not with each one pulling in opposite directions.

Some argue that the period of hyperglobalisation is now over. The distributional effects and the consequent social disruption have already played out and cannot be reversed. There is therefore no longer any imperative to act seeing as the horse has bolted.[22] This argument has two major flaws. The first is that it depends on a level of certainty about future developments that cannot possibly exist. What makes us think that academic economists' predictions of what will happen over the next decades will be any more reliable than their failures to predict the developments of the 1990s?

The second is that it ignores the politics that have arisen around the disruption caused by globalisation. Failure to act is not a viable political option. Being seen to act, on the other hand, leads to potential gains over the electoral cycle, irrespective of the largely unknowable longer-term consequences.

> **Failure to act over global trade is not a viable political option**

Finally, it is as well to make the point that not all evils must be attributed to trade. Company managers who fail to improve training, productivity and to drive innovation are also to blame for falling wages and loss of jobs. Shareholder-focused economies that prioritise short-term financial gains to shareholders over long-term investment will continue to destroy economies.[23] And, of course, the collective failure to ensure financial stability leading to the financial crash and all that went with it.

That said, while these factors must take a fair share of the blame, they must not be used as fig leaves to allow us to continue to ignore the undoubted additional impact of the current trade model.

Are human beings more than just 'consumers'?

In the language of international trade, people are mere 'consumers'. The purpose of open trade is to lower the cost of goods reaching consumers thereby increasing consumption and economic activity. In this world view, anything goes for a penny off. Rather than local production for local consumption (something considered 'inefficient' by some economists), it is considered better to have products travel twice round the globe so that, when they reach the shops, they are cheaper. All else can be subordinated to the ultimate penny off.

> Should we keep believing that anything goes for a penny off?

This might seem to some like a caricature that is not to be taken seriously. The sceptical only need to read a report by Policy Exchange[24], a think tank, about the future of British agriculture post Brexit. Even for an island nation like Britain, the authors take view that *"the first and most important stakeholder in food and farming is the consumer"*.

They use this perspective to go on to argue that cheap food should be the primary objective of policy while concerns such as the food security of an island nation are of little relevance, according to the report.

But are the days of human beings just being reduced to insatiable consumers numbered?

People today care about a lot more. Many are starting to question the environmental cost of all this criss-crossing global trade (global carbon emissions from trade-driven shipping are forecast to increase

People no longer define themselves as mere consumers of mass produced products

by 250 percent by 2050 with no viable means to decarbonise). Tastes are changing as is the appetite for mass produced goods. And at the macro level, we are all wondering how long, in a finite planet, we can persist with an economic model that is based on ever-increasing consumption.

People in developed countries are also less and less willing to accept labour conditions in some production countries. We import agricultural products that are low cost and freely available because of the considerable environmental destruction wrought in the countries in which they are grown. The Amazon forest is being replaced by soy farms. Natural spaces in Indonesia are mown

57

down to make way for palm oil plantations. And so on.

Similarly, climate change regulations have resulted in a significant amount of manufacturing being shipped out to counties that are perfectly happy to keep putting out carbon emissions without constraint – to the detriment of us all. Other goods, including our clothes, smart phones, electric cars and solar panels, are produced using child slave labour in some countries. Rare earths are today's blood diamonds, yet we consume them without constraint.

Social and environmental externalities can no longer be brushed under the table

We have, to date, salved our consciences by referring to international standards that exporting countries should abide by. And that corporations that source product, materials or services from other countries have their own rules and codes of conduct. While we conveniently ignore that these standards are unenforceable and largely ignored – in spite of the weasel words of both corporations and governments when such abuses come to light.

The scale of the problem became clear when Dutch journalist Teun van de Keuken set out to produce chocolate made with cocoa that did not involve child slave labour in its production. After he launched Tony's Chocoloney, he was sued by rivals on the basis that chocolate that was free of slave-labour was simply impossible to produce. This is spite of the Harkin-Engel protocol that had committed all chocolate producers to produce slave-free chocolate by 2005. Teun won the case but it had taken years of effort to achieve his product's promise.

Some recent initiatives, such as The Better Cobalt Pilot, are trying to counter these issues by tracking raw materials all the way along the supply chain. It remains to be seen how effective they will be. Whether they will manage to get beyond what Anneke van Woudenberg, executive director of Rights and Accountability, a UK charity, calls *"nothing more than fluff"* which help offending companies whitewash their image.[25]

Over time, all this will impact the future shape of international trade. It all needs to be taken into account as the nature and shape of globalisation continues to change.

Industry is already moving in new directions

Hamburg G20 communiqué[26], 2017:

> *"Global Supply Chains can be an important source of job creation and balanced economic growth. However, challenges for achieving an inclusive, fair and sustainable globalisation remain,"*

The need for business to maintain the smooth functioning of global supply chains is one of the oft-invoked reasons for maintaining the globalisation momentum. But what is the future of global supply chains? Will they remain as important as they are today?

For many, localisation has replaced globalisation as the contemporary watchword.

Inge Thulin, CEO of 3M:[27]

> *"Our strategy has changed. If you go back several years, there was a strategy of producing at huge facilities at certain places around the world and shipping it to other countries. But now we have a strategy of localisation and regionalisation. We think you should invest in your domestic market as much as you can,"*

'Localisation' has replaced 'globalisation' as the contemporary watchword

Or GE CEO Jeff Immelt:[24]

> *"The days of outsourcing are declining. Chasing the lowest labour costs is yesterday's model,"*

The rise, albeit slowly, of closed loop supply chains (aka a circular economy) will also make geography even more relevant than it has been in the past with widely scattered supply chains becoming less financially viable.

The new digital world also offers fresh challenges – this time related to national security.

Qi Lu, Chief Operating Officer of Chinese internet company Baidu, talks of how autonomous, driverless cars can be hacked and turned into weapons:

> *"The days of building a vehicle in one place and it runs everywhere are over. Because a vehicle that can move by itself by definition it is a weapon."*[28]

Security concerns have also been expressed around trade in communications and digital equipment where manufacturers from foreign countries might have the ability to introduce back door features that create security loopholes. Hence the US has been taking steps to block Huawei – a company with close ties to the Chinese state.

Are security concerns the new barrier to trade?

If we move away from traditional manufacturing industries, then 'localisation' can have different meanings.

Amazon is one of the poster children of the global corporation that has benefited from open trade. Yet it sets up fulfilment centres locally where it operates, employs people locally and maybe even favours local suppliers. What it spectacularly does not do is pay taxes locally – an issue we will come to later.

In an increasingly digital world, we are also seeing the Balkanisation of data – an issue driven by both privacy and security concerns. The EU does not trust others' privacy regulations. The US is concerned about security. And China wishes to maintain total control of information and data flows to and from its citizens. Not the best substrate on which to build an interconnected world of digital commerce.

The text of the Trans-Pacific Partnership Agreement relating to digital commerce illustrates the issues.[29] While the tariff, customs duties and non-discrimination hurdles proved relatively straightforward to negotiate (albeit with yet more exceptions for state aid and subsidies), most of the text deals with standards – from electronic signatures, to privacy, to location of data servers, to use of personal information, and so forth. It is clear from the text that such issues remain fully under the control of each individual country. All the agreement manages to achieve is a vague encouragement of greater cooperation.

Neo-mercantilism is back in vogue

Mercantilism in the traditional sense was supposed to have disappeared centuries ago. As the ideology of totally free and unfettered markets took hold in the latter half of the twentieth century, mercantilism's offspring, neo-mercantilism, was also heavily frowned upon – at least in the public rhetoric.

Neo-mercantilism – the practice of focusing on achieving a trade surplus and the use of capital controls and centralized currency decisions – became equated with 'protectionism'. Those who supported free and open markets argued that this damaged consumer welfare.

The reality is that, in spite of the public pronouncements, the mercantilist mentality never really disappeared. Some argue that the best mercantilist countries are simply the best at hiding behind the rhetoric of free trade. It comes as no surprise that China and Germany – the two countries with the largest sustained trade surpluses – are currently the most vocal defenders of free trade. China now accounts for a whopping 13 per cent of all exports. Germany, aided by a euro that effectively gives it a relative currency devaluation, persists in riding roughshod over EU rules by maintaining what is considered an excessive trade surplus with its consequent destabilising effect. It refuses to take measure to stimulate local consumption.

And, to cap it all, China and Germany are the two countries that have implemented the greatest number of restrictive trade interventions in the last decade (see figure on p.72).

Is defence of open trade merely the rhetoric of mercantilist countries?

We should all take German and Chinese exhortations in favour of free trade with a large pinch of salt.

While it is probably true that a mercantilist mentality that focuses on ever greater accumulation of reserves at the expense of others is unhealthy and damaging, the converse is also the case. No country can reasonably sustain perpetual trade deficits.

Countries with perpetual trade deficits need to pay for those deficits somehow. The options available are mainly foreign debt and foreign investment to purchase domestic assets. Both of these are potentially problematic if sustained indefinitely. They, too, imply a significant loss of sovereignty to foreign interests – whether those interests are unelected and unaccountable commercial interests or whether they represent the long arm of foreign states exercising influence through sovereign wealth funds or state-controlled corporations. Perpetual trade deficits convert countries into economic colonies of others – a situation that we all saw play out as we watched with horror the total subjugation and impoverishment of Greece and the Greek people at the hands of their so-called European 'partners'.

In the US, these issues may be less marked because of the dollar's position as the world's reserve currency. But that may well change over time.

In a world where countries oscillate between carrying trade deficits some of the time and benefiting from trade surpluses at other times, then the deficit-surplus issue need not be an insurmountable problem. But when so many countries are now perpetually in deficit, a correction is inevitable.

Not all trade is trade

In evaluating the benefits of trade, it is important that we focus on actual trade. By that we mean the flow of goods and services.

Yet many so-called 'trade agreements' now explicitly include capital account liberalisation – in other words they require the free flow of capital as part of the agreement. This is not what we, the authors, understand by 'trade' – even though such liberalisation is often slipped in under the false guise of liberalising financial services. Most economists are now sceptical about the benefits of uncontrolled capital flows. They are seen to contribute to destabilisation and financial crises and to limit governments' abilities to deal effectively with such crises. *"There is...no presumption that full liberalisation [of capital flows] is an appropriate goal for all countries at all times"* according to the IMF[30].

Recognising the potentially destabilising impact of large capital flows, the IMF view is now that capital controls can serve to protect economies in certain circumstances.[31] It is also worth noting that, in spite of continued pressure from the US and others, China has not fully liberalised its capital account – maybe wisely.

Apart from the issues with financial stability, liberalisation of capital flows facilitates industrial scale tax arbitrage as well as money laundering activities. Unabashed tax arbitrage by multinational corporations, and especially, though not exclusively, technology companies, has been one of the main drivers of the backlash against globalisation.

In opposing a UK proposal to tax such companies on local revenues rather than locally booked profits, Russ Shaw, Founder of Tech London Advocates and Global Tech Advocates perfectly illustrates the bankruptcy of arguments in support of tax arbitrage. He makes an empty nod to the idea that *"the biggest multinational tech firms have a responsibility to contribute a fair and adequate level of tax"* – without in any way suggesting how that might be achieved.

Uncontrolled capital flows are destabilising and cause many of the perceived problems with globalisation

He then goes on to provide the only justification against a crackdown: *"It is therefore imperative that the UK remains an attractive destination for large investment... at a time when other European cities are gaining appeal."*[32]   In other words, the only available justification is international tax competition and the threat to disinvest. It does not seem to occur to Mr Shaw that persisting in these arguments threatens to undermine the very foundations of globalisation.

In reviewing the future shape of globalisation, it is therefore imperative that we separate what we might call 'real trade' from capital flows. The latter may have become problematic.

Going forward, it is doubtful whether liberalisation of capital movement should be routinely included in free trade agreements. The nature, risks and benefits of trade are fundamentally different compared to capital flows. They should

> **Capital account liberalisation should be excluded from future trade agreements**

therefore be treated differently. Arguably, it is the liberalisation of capital flows, not trade, that is the biggest driver of the issues we are seeing with globalization, and the consequent backlash.

The emerging market perspective

It can reasonably be argued that much of what we have written so far represents a developed market perspective. What of emerging markets (EMs) and their view of world trade?

As we have outlined, EMs, and particularly those in Asia, have been the primary beneficiaries of international trade. Largely it is those countries that have combined trading ability with governance structures that make sure that the benefits of international trade are converted into positive development of their people and their countries rather than being frittered away or concentrated among a handful of powerful rulers and their protégés.

But the relationship is under strain.

EMs still feel under-represented in global governance structures. Developed markets, on the other hand, risk starting to change how they see some of the advantages that emerging markets had to offer – such as lower labour costs – from 'comparative advantage' to 'unfair competition.' Similarly, and as we mentioned previously, concerns about working conditions and environmental damage continue to rise and become increasingly politically damaging.

China is using its considerable cash reserves to invest in emerging markets – from its Belt and Road initiative, to securing mining rights for rare earths, to building control over infrastructure ranging from trans-African railroads to the port of Piraeus in Greece. Other countries are participating in some of this through membership of the Asian

> **No other country can currently match China's investment in emerging markets**

Infrastructure Investment Bank. But no other country currently has the financial heft to match China's expansion. A financial heft that results from – guess what – a huge and sustained trade surplus.

Recognising the new world of trading blocs, African countries are trying to forge a common market through the Tripartite Free Trade Area that brings together what were previously three different African trading blocs. This is further evolving into a wider African Continental Free Trade Area with forty-four signatories. So far, the aim is to create a continental free trade area. Nigeria, Africa's largest economy, and ten other countries have opted not to sign up. It remains to be seen what shape this new bloc will take and its role in global trade outside of its own African market.

People in emerging markets equate "free trade" with the right to export

The outlook for EMs is complex. International trade under the current regime has brought them financial wealth. But, as developed markets find themselves increasingly under strain, it is not clear that the outlook is as positive as it has been in the past.

Given that EMs have, in recent years, been the main beneficiaries of international trade, it is not surprising that the majority of the populations in EMs still see globalisation as a force for good – in sharp contrast to people in developed markets whose views are becoming more jaded.[33]

But we should not take such results at face value. When asked in the same survey whether their countries should be self-sufficient or rely on imports, most respondents in Indonesia, Thailand, India, the Philippines and Malaysia feel that their countries should not have to rely on imports. People in EMs do not, it seems, actually support full liberalisation. They support only that which makes them wealthier – exporting their goods.

It is uncertain whether developed markets will give EMs more voice in global governance bodies. Maybe we shouldn't be holding our breath for that to happen. But it is likely that any significant breakdown in the international system will, in the current state of affairs, hurt EMs more than developed markets. This puts EMs in a difficult position – between trying to assert themselves to make sure that a trading structure that benefits them is maintained, and risking being shut out as developed markets turn inwards to face their own mounting problems.

For the moment, China can act as the white knight. How long that will last, and how EMs will come to view that relationship a few years down the road remains a matter for speculation.

So, what is happening to trade?

If our analysis above has any merit at all, then we should expect to see more interventions designed to restrict trade and, eventually, a slowdown, if not slow reversal, of international trade flows.

At the political level, the evidence of a swing away from unfettered globalisation is certainly clear for all to see – from China's policies described above, to Trump's pugilistic approach to trade, to the EU's inward-looking perspective that prioritises its own single market over everything else – as is becoming ever clearer in the Brexit negotiations. The three major trading blocs are diverging in their policy priorities and trade policy will likely diverge with these priorities.

Since 2009, the number of interventions that have a restricting effect on trade has far outstripped those that further liberalise trade (top figure, p 72). Again, it seems that it is China and Germany – the countries with the most vocal pro-trade rhetoric at the last G20 – that have, in reality, applied the largest number of restricting measures.

In terms of trade volumes themselves, the most recent WTO review shows that world trade as a ratio of global GDP has shown a sustained slowdown over the last few years (bottom figure, p 72) – and even before the full effects of the Trump phenomenon have yet come into play.

"The further slowing of trade relative to GDP remains a cause for concern," according to the WTO.

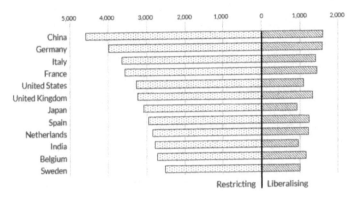

Total number of interventions that affect trade
by country, 2009-2018

Source: Global Trade Alert

International trade as a proportion of global GDP
has recently slowed down

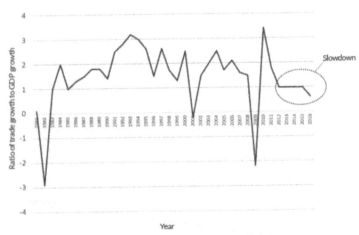

Source: World Trade Organisation. World Trade Statistical Review 2017

Rather than limiting ourselves to expressing concern, we have tried in this section to lay out how a changing world inevitably will continue to have an impact on how people and nations view international trade.

Given that changing world, what is surprising to us is that the slowdown has not been greater.

We find it surprising that the slowdown in trade has not been greater

It may yet be so if nations and major trading blocs evolve the view that more trade under the current structures no longer serves their domestic or foreign policy priorities.

Yet the limited slowdown may also be a sign of the resilience of trade to being buffeted by multiple events. In spite of the obstacles, eventually, one could argue, people will find ways of trading with each other.

But now is not the time for complacency. For sitting back and hoping that it will all simply come right in the end. The backlash against globalisation will not simply evaporate and neither will the political impact of a growing discontent.

The business world is already moving past what are now considered outdated notions of what globalisation should mean. Politics will, as usual, take some time to catch up. But it gives us a glimmer

Now is not the time for policy complacency

of hope that some may be open to exploring new kinds of trade arrangements. We might one day look forward to a different understanding of free trade – one that was more in tune with its roots. This is the subject of our next section.

3

A new look for international trade

"I was brought up to believe that there is no virtue in conforming meekly to the dominant opinion of the moment. I was encouraged to believe that simple conformity results in stagnation for a society. Progress has been achieved largely owing to the opportunity for experimentation, the leeway given to initiative and the gusto and a freedom for chewing over odd ideas."

Jane Jacobs

We have argued that the consequences of free trade deals in their late twentieth century form is causing a backlash against globalisation that threatens to throw free trade into reverse. We agree with the IMF and others that such an outcome would be undesirable. Where we differ is that the status quo supported by a change in national policies is the only option. We believe that it is time for a discussion on what new forms of trade arrangements could look like. Arrangements that sustain the original purpose of free trade while reducing or eliminating the now obvious downsides.

Our suggestions are based on the following principles:

- Trade policy that fits within an overall policy framework.

- Flexibility and incrementalism rather than attempts at catch-all trade agreements.

- A focus on helping small and medium sized enterprises rather than only large multinational firms.

- A focus on trade rather than investment.

- A trade structure that encourages innovation rather than oligopoly.

- Favouring the building of cultural links.

We will address each of these issues in turn. But first a look at the general framework of global trade in terms of tariffs and regulations.

Tariffs and regulation

There are two basic hurdles to frictionless free trade across borders: tariffs and regulatory standards.

Tariffs are not currently the major issue

Between 1996 and 2013, average tariffs applied by WTO members have declined by 15 per cent. Most

WTO members apply tariffs at rates that are significantly lower than the upper bound allowed by the WTO (Figure). The average tariff applied by WTO members is now a mere 9 per cent. In short, tariffs, today, are nowhere near the barrier to trade that they used to be.

Applied tariffs are well below WTO Bound rates

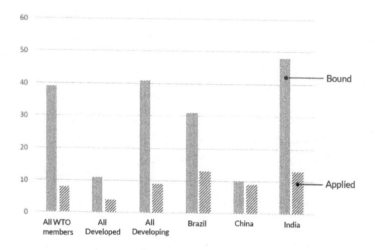

Source: WTO, World Tariff Profiles

That said, whether it is viable to maintain such a low tariff world, or reduce tariffs further, is a different question altogether.

There will always be legitimate reasons to apply some tariffs – whether to protect against dumping tactics, or to compensate for asymmetric state aid, or to support domestic industries, such as defence, that are considered of strategic importance.

Many see tariffs as being like a safety valve for international trade. If trade is perceived to be working smoothly, then most countries will work to continue mutually to reduce or eliminate tariffs. But, tariffs are the easiest and quickest tool to reach for under pressure – as Mr Trump is demonstrating.

> Tariffs are seen as the safety valve of the international trade system

In the complex interwoven world of international trade, the impact of increased tariffs ends up being somewhat unpredictable and never quite as expected. Yet, they are a political tool as much as a tool of international trade.

Of course, the indiscriminate or inappropriate use of safety valves when they are not necessary causes problems. Similarly, tariffs can be abused. The unilateral imposition of tariffs raises all sorts of hackles and invites retaliation. Are tariffs being imposed for reasons that most would consider reasonable and legitimate? Or not? These questions will never be resolved to perfection. Rather than the fact of tariffs themselves, it is, maybe the unilateral imposition of tariffs that is the most disruptive.

However, those who oppose the unilateral imposition of tariffs need to come up with practical alternatives. Decades-long multilateral discussions with everyone spouting hypocritical free trade rhetoric while fiercely defending their own national self-interest does not present a credible way forward.

In short, tariffs need not be classified as either 'a good thing' or a 'bad thing'. Tariffs are a tool of policy. As with all tools, they can be used well or abused. What matters more is the general environment under which international trade is being conducted, and whether countries act unilaterally or within an agreed framework. If trade is fulfilling domestic and foreign policy objectives for most countries, then many will continue to work to reduce tariffs and encourage trade. If trade is seen to be working against national interests, then one can expect tariffs to be increasingly deployed. Currently, we might well be finding ourselves in the latter environment.

Tariffs will rise if trade is seen as failing to fulfil domestic or foreign policy objectives

Regulatory standards are the knotty issue of world trade

Rather than tariffs, it is differing regulatory standards that, today, constitute the largest barrier to trade. Here things get much more difficult since regulatory standards are driven by cultural values and the shaping of social and economic life in the pursuit of those values.

As international trade lawyer Robert McDougall points out, the challenge is to integrate regulation to make trade as frictionless as possible while having countries or trading blocs maintain the autonomy to regulate their societies in a way that reflects local values. *"Striking that balance is the true holy grail of international integration."*[34]

Based on these observations, we put forward below some suggestions as to opportunities to improve the framework under which international trade is conducted - to make it more appropriate for current needs and, maybe, for the future.

Trade policy cannot stand alone

As we have outlined previously, for some, the view has grown that, because trade provides a net increase in 'welfare', then policy must be focused on encouraging international trade and domestic policy must align with that objective in order to mitigate the adverse effects of globalisation. We reject this formulation of the issue. In our view, it looks at the world the wrong way around.

It is true – and important to recognise – that trade policy cannot stand alone. Its impact on other areas of policy is substantial. It is therefore vital that trade policy does not run in isolation but develops in tandem with other areas of policy to ensure alignment.

Yet we believe that trade policy should be seen as an instrument of countries' domestic and foreign policies. In other words, countries need to formulate their trade policies to achieve their domestic and foreign policy

> International trade is an instrument of domestic and foreign policy

goals not, as some suggest, the other way around. The trade tail cannot be the one to wag the domestic and foreign policy dog.

And, in general, it does not – and never has. As we outlined in our introductory chapter, trade policy has always oscillated between more liberalisation and more restrictiveness. That oscillation has been driven by the policy agenda in other areas. When open trade contributes to those policy goals, it has been pursued. When domestic or foreign policy goals seem to demand the erection of trade barriers, they have been erected. Of course, whether trade liberalisation or restriction ends up actually achieving the desired domestic goals is a question for debate.

In summary:

"[it may be] a misnomer to [persist in calling] these "trade" agreements. All national policy can in some way or another affect trade and what we need are cooperation agreements that allow to take into account effect on trade of policies that are, at least in the first

instance, designed to regulate the national economy and society."[35]

The main policy environment facing many developed countries today is one of relative economic decline, rising inequality among their populations and, in foreign affairs, a polarisation into three power blocs, plus a potential Russia/Iran/Turkey alliance, all trying to assert their own spheres of influence. Europe and the US have for some time used trade policy to assert their foreign policy goals. They will continue to do so.

From that perspective, some form of trade confrontation between China and the US may well be inevitable as the US defends its interests in the face of Chinese expansionism.

A trade confrontation between the US and China may well be inevitable

Given that, over the last 500 years, in twelve out of sixteen cases where a rising power has threatened a ruling power it has led to armed conflict,[36] a trade war may be a small price to pay compared to the alternative.

But a layer of complexity has been added in that the current form of globalisation is now being seen in the developed West as being inimical to domestic policy objectives by enabling de-industrialisation, rising inequality and cultural disruption. If we are not to see a progressive withdrawal from international trade, at least for a while, then the basis on which we do trade must change. We must try to find ways in which trade is seen to alleviate rather than augment these domestic political issues.

This is what we turn our attention to next.

1. Strengthening competition policy

We start our recommendations with something that may, at first sight, have little to do with global trade – competition policy.

As we outlined earlier, industrially, the net effect of global trade has been to strengthen those that can operate globally. It has facilitated the ability of larger corporations to build oligopolistic or monopolistic market positions that competition authorities have been either unable or unwilling to tackle. This is further encouraged by the open approach that some countries, the UK notable among them, have taken to merger and acquisition activity – both in-country and cross-border.

It goes without saying that such developments risk stifling innovation, sinking us all into rentier economies and, eventually, turn our democracies into plutocracies. Some believe that we are already there on all three counts.

It is true that most trade negotiators (and their political masters) don't set out to sign deals that encourage oligopoly, but rather to promote innovation through competition and constraints on state action that supports domestic oligopolies. The result, though, may be that powerful corporate interests are able to lobby for features that give them advantage. Or just that economies of scale, without effective co-operation on anti-trust, allow the emergence of oligopolies.[37]

> *"As always, consumers are politically less powerful than producers, as their per capita losses are smaller than the producers' per capita gains, and they face more barriers to collective action."*[38]

In a recent article in American Conservative[39], Daniel Kishi traces the emasculation of anti-trust to Robert Bork and his book *The Anti-Trust Paradox* (1978). The book had a significant impact on thinking in the Anglo-Saxon world. In the forty years since its publication, corporate concentration has soared. In the USA, *"three drug stores control 99 percent of their market; four airlines control 80 percent of the domestic aviation market; and two companies, Facebook and Google, control 75 percent of the digital advertising market. And the trend is continuing, from agriculture to health insurers, defense contractors to beer,"* according to Kishi.

Competition policy and international trade are no longer separable

The current EU investigations into the dominance of digital giants such as Google and Facebook highlight the relationship between trade and competition policy.

While the EU sees its actions as a matter of competition policy, the US government protests that such investigations amount to trade protectionism.

It is beyond the scope of this book to make recommendations around competition policy. We will return to this issue in a subsequent publication. Here suffice it to say that without a significant strengthening of competition policy, and its vigorous enforcement, international trade cannot work effectively. Its adverse effects will continue to grow, and popular opinion, and, consequently, political action, will become ever more anti-globalist.

An inevitable corollary of this line of argument is that, as we have indicated previously, there must be some degree of constraint in the movement of capital (as China has shown), echoing part of the previously quoted statement by J.M. Keynes: *"above all, let finance be primarily national."*

Absent significant strengthening of anti-trust action, popular opinion will become ever more anti-globalist

While here we mention only competition policy, we have indicated previously the reality that the more one liberalises trade, the more other areas, not only competition policy but also tax, social benefits, immigration, etc., are affected. Addressing trade agreements in isolation without paying heed to their wider consequences has been one of the causes of the issues that have arisen and the subsequent backlash.

2. Realism, flexibility and incrementalism: mutual recognition arrangements

Trade deals can become fiendishly complex, take years to negotiate and often over-reach into areas that are not necessary for trade. The complexity of the current approach was recently recognised by Dr. Liam Fox, UK Secretary of State for International Trade who, in October 2017, promised that the UK would replicate up to 40 of the 60 or so EU trade deals to be ready for *"one second after midnight"* on March 29 2019, to make sure that there was *"no disruption"* to trade.

But, now faced with reality, Dr Fox has finally conceded that it is not as simple as *"cut and pasting"* the EU's existing deals to create bilateral UK equivalents.[40] Indeed, if the cut and paste approach were to be followed, the UK would gain precisely nothing from its new-found ability to be more flexible in its trade negotiations than if it had remained in the EU.

The twentieth century approach is reminiscent of another, now obsolete, twentieth century practice – the 'waterfall' approach to software development projects. A big, all-singing, all-dancing IT project is defined. It takes years to implement comprehensively (by which time requirements have changed), goes significantly over-budget and rarely, if ever, works as advertised.

We take our cue instead from the new approach of agile development: adaptive planning, evolutionary development, early delivery, continuous improvement, and rapid and flexible response to change.

What would this mean for a modern trade deal?

It would mean replacing the all-encompassing trade deal with a sector-by-sector approach starting with those sectors where regulatory standards are close, and tariffs are low, non-existent or not material. Other sectors can, if appropriate, be added later.

It is important to clarify that what we are advocating is mutual recognition arrangements NOT regulatory harmonisation as, for example, practiced in the European Single Market. Mutual recognition accepts,

Platform agreements based on mutual recognition will encourage innovation and experimentation

even encourages, somewhat differing regulatory approaches provided that the outcomes are not felt to be materially different. This encourages experimentation, innovation and the emergence of different approaches.

Over time, countries can learn from others' experiences and see which approach works best. Further, it need not impose new regulatory standards on the non-traded part of the economy – a situation that disadvantages local producers who do not trade internationally.

EU harmonisation, on the other hand, is a one-size-fits-all approach that created an unnecessary bureaucracy to harmonise rules even where differences were immaterial. It is one of the factors that has given the EU its reputation for pettifogging regulation.

Harmonisation also stifles innovation since, hemmed in by a single set of rules, nobody can try anything new and the opportunity for experimentation is therefore killed. Further a poorly designed regulation (there will always be those in spite of everyone's best efforts) ends up being imposed on a whole continent. Whether one trades outside one's borders or not, nobody can escape harmonisation. And changing poor regulation (take the Common Agricultural Policy as one example) with the agreement of all EU member states has proven well-nigh impossible or, at best, a decades long process.

Another downside of the EU's harmonisation approach is that, progressively, the Union risks becoming in the eyes of some a Union of coercion rather than one of co-operation willingly given. If that view takes hold, it may well undermine the Union irretrievably.

Our approach would, instead, call for countries to negotiate "framework" or "platform" agreements that would not try to be all encompassing but rather provide a scaffolding on which more can be built over time and at a pace that works for all partners. Discussions will be largely between regulatory agencies that will be tasked with determining what needs to be done to make mutual recognition possible among different regulatory approaches.

This requires somewhat of a change in mindset among regulators. They will need to abandon the idea that their own particular regulatory frameworks are always 'the best' and show an openness to learn from what others have done. The objective needs to be to construct open dialogue over the long term and a determination to find ways to bridge differences. Such a dialogue could, if well managed, bring countries together and build mutual understanding in more ways than simply enhancing trade.

There is, of course, nothing new about the idea of mutual recognition (MR) of standards. Different technical names have been used for small

> **We need to seek open dialogue amongst open minds**

differences in approach – equivalence, alignment, etc. Though the fundamental idea has been around for some time, it has not, to date, been pushed as the mainstay of trade agreements. MR of Good Laboratory Practice for pharmaceutical products has been established for some time but never extended to product licencing.

The EU tried to explore MR during the Transatlantic Trade and Investment Partnership discussions but largely got nowhere. The closest we have got to it so far is the Trans-Tasman Mutual Recognition Arrangement between Australia and New Zealand. This has been criticised for excluding a number of sectors. But that is precisely what we are proposing – In the words of Francis of Assisi *"Start by doing what's necessary; then do what's possible; and suddenly you are doing the impossible."*

Trade in services

Are the issues more challenging when it comes to trade in services? It is possible to imagine MR agreements that cover defined goods. Goods tend to have defined specifications that can be documented, and agreement reached, or not, as to whether such specifications, and any changes to them, are mutually acceptable to trading partners. Further, manufacturers can adapt their product to fit the requirements of other jurisdictions.

Mutual recognition of services requires a higher level of trust

Some, though not all, services, on the other hand, can be more complex. Services are more changeable, and their regulation usually requires ongoing close supervision rather than one-off approval. MR therefore requires a level of trust between regulators that ongoing supervisory regimes are fit for purpose, well thought out, and well enforced.

These are some of the reasons why services have, to date, proven to be less tradeable than goods. We suggest that focusing on the MR approach may offer an avenue where an increase in trade in services might be achievable over time. For instance, MR of professional qualifications already happens in some sectors across some countries. There is no reason why this cannot be extended much further.

Where there is more work to do is in financial services and digital commerce.

Financial services

Some argue that financial services are a problematic area because of their impact on financial stability. For this reason, individual jurisdictions want to maintain their own supervisory regimes.

But this gets back to the question we posed earlier. Is financial stability truly a factor in the trade of financial services? Or does it arise from the free movement of

Trade in financial services needs to be kept separate from international capital flows

capital that often accompanies what are generally called 'financial services'? According to an IMF paper:

> "The removal or restrictions on international capital movements and the opening of the domestic financial sector to foreign competition are two interrelated, yet distinct, components of international financial liberalisation."[41]

Yet the two are often confused or treated as one.

The above quoted paper shows that there are many varying impacts depending on the type of financial service that is traded and the amount of capital flow. It concludes:

> "The findings underscore the need for differentiating the design of international financial liberalisation between capital movement and trade in financial services, and, within the latter, across different types of financial services and modes of trading them."

We therefore suggest that it is time that we abandon the practice of treating 'financial services' as an all-encompassing term. Future trade agreements will need to

(i) divide financial services into their different sectors, and
(ii) treat trade in services separately from capital flows. If trade in services is separated from capital flows, the issues

associated with financial stability become less of a concern. MR of financial services provided across borders becomes less problematic.

Digital commerce

The rise of the internet economy, AI, and digital commerce will likely make many more services (from business services, to education, to medical services) potentially tradable. But we are still some way away from agreeing common standards that cover issues relating to data privacy and security.

While the text of the Trans-Pacific Partnership Agreement illustrates the issues, it also maybe provides a template of what a broad 'framework' or 'platform' agreement would look like. The Agreement does not resolve many issues definitively, but it lays the ground for longer term co-operation and convergence.

> For digital commerce it is possible that no other approach could be effective other than a framework agreement to work towards mutual recognition

Reading through the Agreement, it becomes clear that:

- Regulatory issues are the key constraint,

- The aim is to have countries work towards common, or at least compatible, regulatory standards, and

- Regulatory control ultimately rests within each individual country.

For instance, the text on personal privacy goes like this:

"Recognising that the Parties may take different legal approaches to protecting personal information, each Party should encourage the development of mechanisms to promote compatibility between these different regimes. These mechanisms may include the recognition of regulatory outcomes, whether accorded autonomously or by mutual arrangement, or broader international frameworks. To this end, the Parties shall endeavour to exchange information on any such mechanisms applied in their jurisdictions and explore ways to extend these or other suitable arrangements to promote compatibility between them."

Essentially, this is a statement of intent to work towards mutually recognised regulatory arrangements. It will take time. There will likely be many hiccups. But in the world of digital commerce, it is doubtful whether there are any other viable ways forward.

What other issues arise?

Some argue that the weakness of a sector-by-sector approach is the loss of negotiating ability that allows trade-offs between sectors. You give something in this sector and, in return, I give you something in another sector. Some further argue that limiting the flexibility offered by such trade-offs will strengthen the negotiating power of larger players relative to smaller ones.

This is an important line of argument. But the reality is that, when they are advantageous, trade-offs will still be possible since, over time, framework agreements will cut across many sectors and many aspects of trade.

A further area fraught with difficulty is the question of what some choose to call 'social and environmental dumping'. In the previous chapter we referred to the social and environmental externalities associated with international trade and the difficulties in managing them. Of course, what may be seen as social and environmental dumping by some can be considered the only source of comparative advantage by others. Yet more to debate around Ricardo's theory.

Much work has been done to develop some internationally accepted standards. Civil society has also worked hard to improve the situation through Fair Trade and other certification schemes. But standards are still, in general, poorly monitored and often un-enforced. They do, however, provide importing countries with an agreed set of benchmarks against which to judge whether to import goods or services from countries that do not meet agreed standards.

We are still to find effective approaches to the social and environmental consequences of trade

This is likely to be an area of continued tension in international trade; one that will probably not disappear for decades to come. Once again, framework agreements focused on working towards mutually recognised standards over time could, at the very least, open up this darker side of international trade to more public debate. While recognising, of course, that that is the last thing that some interests would like to see happening, it is an aspect of future trade arrangements that cannot be ignored.

***

Overall, we believe that our suggested MR approach seeks to be realistic and honest while looking to replace mega-trade deals with agile incrementalism.

It is realistic in that it focuses primarily on regulatory hurdles rather than tariffs. We look for incrementalism using the basic principle that not everything needs to be done at once. Framework agreements go for the quick wins that do not upset the current regulatory regimes and build further wins over time as regulatory standards converge. This approach provides an incentive for convergence without coercion and without trading countries imposing the values inherent in regulatory standards on each other.

Much of it is a question of mindset. Framework agreements are designed to be flexible and adaptable to changing circumstances. Both TPP and CETA are essentially statements of principles and intent to cooperate to achieve regulatory alignment over time. In a rapidly changing world, that is how trade will evolve.

3. Focus on small and medium-sized enterprises

Our suggested approach above helps all types of companies. But its positive effect will be disproportionately beneficial to micro, small and medium-sized enterprises (MSMEs).

Large corporations have the resources and wherewithal to deal with multiple regulatory agencies across the world. It's a cost, but they can manage it. For SMEs, on the other hand, mutual recognition would significantly lower the burden of international trade. A small French company could work with its local regulator for approval of its product or service and, having cleared that hurdle, would immediately have access beyond its borders.

Initiatives to help SMEs

Trade policy for the past half century has ended up favouring large scale enterprises over smaller ones – largely unintentionally. Partly this is due to the greater lobbying power and campaign contributions of larger firms that have allowed them to steer negotiations to their advantage. Partly it is due to an inherent assumption that it is only larger entities that can manage cross-border trade effectively and that they therefore constitute the best channels for the projection of economic power. And partly it is due to a belief in the benefits of economies of scale.

Global trade today has the potential to stimulate the growth of MSMEs

Apart from the persistence, and probably the increase, of lobbying power, none of these assumptions hold true any longer. In today's digital marketplace, world markets are open to SMEs in a way that they never were before.

It has become increasingly apparent to policy-makers and, as we outlined earlier, to corporations themselves, that – once you see the whole picture – economies of scale are very rapidly dwarfed by diseconomies of scale. Today, global trade therefore has the potential to stimulate the growth of the economic base provided by MSMEs – companies that account for at least half of all economic activity.

To achieve this, we suggest some incremental activities:

- Cross-border agencies jointly funded by both governments, with interfaces in both nations to provide help and end-to-end guidance on accessing international markets

- Each country to provide capital to finance SME access to international markets

These initiatives would focus on making cross-border deals possible for private companies, B-corps or community interest companies of less than 200 employees. They will provide advice, support and heft to break through red tape and find investors for deals, primarily but not entirely online.

While there has been a huge explosion in international money flows, international finance is not set up to provide finance for MSMEs. That is not its business. MSMEs are maybe another example of the 'left behind' of globalisation in finance. This is a market failure that needs filling. How it is to be filled will vary from country to country.

Some, like Germany, have a network of local banks that can provide such financing – and they do so at below commercial rates while being protected from takeover. Export guarantee schemes and other forms of government support are also available. But it may also be time to review the structure of state aid limitations that exist in most trade agreements.

Are state aid rules as currently devised too restrictive? Should there be better provision for finding ways to encourage better financing of MSMEs in circumstances of market failure?

Of course, as with anything at all to do with trade, everything can be open to abuse. Some will argue that governments should not be trying to pick winners (though the idea that venture capital firms or banks are much better than appropriately structured public entities at picking winners is largely an article of faith and ideology rather than empirical evidence).

Intervention to make up for market failure in MSME financing needs to be allowed for in trade agreements

It is also argued that any company financed in one country at below market rates gains an unfair competitive advantage over other, potentially better companies in countries that do not provide such aid.

All worthy arguments. The reality is that market failure does exist in many countries in terms of financing available to MSMEs and that intervening in such market failure is probably essential if the MSME sector is to thrive and gain an increasing presence in international trade. We suggest that such practical considerations should inform future trade agreements more than theoretical economic arguments.

4. Prioritise business and trade over investment

We have covered previously the need to separate trade from capital flows. The same distinction applies to separating trade from investment.

While we do not believe that investment should be discouraged, we do not believe that it should be subject to any special protection – and certainly no protection that limits the rights of sovereign governments to regulate. Investment carries risk and it is the investors' responsibility to understand the risks they take in investing in foreign countries.

> **Investor state dispute systems are falling out of favour and should be eliminated**

We would therefore shun investor protection and investor-state dispute systems (ISDS) or any other secret court. These mechanisms are slowly falling out of favour in any case as their effects become more obvious and as corporations dig even deeper to try to use ISDS to protect obsolete or unacceptable business practices. It is time that these mechanisms were consigned to the dustbin of history once and for all.

5. Should trade agreements target trade balances between countries?

We have argued previously that persistent trade imbalances poison relationships between countries and are economically and politically unsustainable. Yet trade agreements are usually silent on trade balances.

One exception is the EU that mandates a six percent maximum surplus – a limit that Germany continues to exceed and which the European Commission has promised to investigate (we'll see), while Germany continues to defend its position.

> **Is it time to ask whether we should place limits on persistent trade imbalances?**

So, it might be time to pose the question: if we are to sustain widespread support for the global trading system, should one work towards some sort of international agreement that seeks to limit persistent, one-way trade imbalances? Free market believers will balk at such a suggestion. Yet, both the politics and the economics of persistent trade imbalances are now clear for all to see. As is the fact that, if allowed to persist or grow, they will likely undermine the whole edifice on which international trade is built.

How to resolve these issues is not obvious. But it might be time to start having the conversation. It may be that the only choice available is either to devise some kind of internationally agreed mechanism to address persistent trade imbalances or else to let every country react to them independently based on the domestic political environment.

6. Prioritise cultural exchange and new thinking

Cultural exchange and cross-fertilisation of thinking are some of the main benefits of globalisation. It could be argued that making sure that different peoples understand each other better is a much more effective route to peace and harmony among nations than de-personalised trade.

Yet there are reasons, political and economic, why complete freedom of movement does not provide the answer at the moment. 'Importing' countries end up relying on foreign labour rather than investing in building their own skills. 'Exporting' countries, on the other hand, suffer a brain drain that prevents

> Cultural exchange may be more important than trade in enhancing understanding and harmony among nations

them from accelerating their own development. In Europe, unlimited freedom of movement has been destabilising and has ended up poisoning the politics of Europe.

Our new trade deal would therefore prioritise cultural exchange and allow the free movement of people via educational and cultural institutions. Doing this will require some kind of funding mechanism that will allow cultural institutions to be involved side by side with the those of other nations. This will be a second trade deal institution, perhaps a department of the other one.

In addition, we would argue for a further opening up of work visas, maybe temporary, at all levels, and in tandem with our previous suggestion of mutual recognition of professional and vocational qualifications.

Leisure travel has exploded in recent years. But people need to live together and work together if they are to develop mutual understanding and learn from each other's different world views. A managed flow of people should therefore be part of every future agreement.

Time for renewal

Traditional trade negotiators may recoil when faced with this agenda.

It is certainly intended to broaden our current understanding of free trade which we believe has not managed to achieve fully the original intention. Our scheme is based on the original understanding that free trade is a concept that supports challengers and drives innovation while supporting countries' own core values, delivering widespread benefits and maintaining social cohesion. Trade should not be a crowbar to enforce compulsory trade, and not a feather bed to protect investors from social values and oligopolies from competition.

We recognise that these last outcomes have never been the intention of any free trade agreement. But, in a messy real world of asymmetric power and government capture by powerful interests, this is the direction that they have ended up following.

We need to re-focus on the original purpose of free trade if globalisation is to regain popular and political support

We believe that for free trade and globalisation to regain popular and political support, trade arrangements need to re-focus on the original conception of trade. Trade as a tool of domestic and foreign policy. To provide benefit to the whole population without compromising their values or ways of life; and to buttress the small against the big. And it needs to be done in practical, incremental and flexible ways that do not undermine democratic institutions. That is what we have set out here.

That we have moved away from this conception of trade is maybe illustrated by the EU's campaign about the benefits of CETA. The campaign focused exclusively on the benefits to various EU exporters and did not make one single mention of benefits to EU citizens.

We also believe that essential to success is an acceptance that trade deals must have limits. Those who argue for totally open doors on the basis that this is not a zero-sum game and the pie can grow ever larger to everyone's benefit have been proven wrong – or, at the very least, that analysis has been shown to be superficial and highly inadequate.

Finally, we cannot get away from the fact that large and persistent unidirectional trade imbalances are not sustainable. Not politically, not socially, and not economically. How to achieve more equitable trade balances over a cycle must become one of the considerations in future trade agreements. If this issue is not seriously addressed, we believe that the future for global trade will be bleak.

Nearly 76 years ago, in August 1941, Churchill and Roosevelt met on board the battleship *Prince of Wales* off the Canadian coast and signed a statement of joint purpose. It was called the Atlantic Charter. One of its stated objectives was global co-operation to secure better economic and social conditions for all. Reduction of trade restrictions was one of the tools to be employed in pursuit of those goals.

There is now little doubt that, following a period of post-war success, the current trade system is falling short of achieving these goals. In its current conception, it may work against some of them. A polarising rather than co-operative world now further risks bringing the whole edifice crumbling down.

It seems unlikely that there is, today, much opportunity for the UK prime minister and the US president to repeat the 1941 trick, at least for the kind of trade deal we set out here. But one day, with different incumbents, if Brexit goes ahead, there will be a new Charter going beyond the Atlantic that can redirect global trade in a whole new, positive and creative direction, boost the status and performance of their diverse and creative small business sectors, break the power of large incumbents, and redirect wealth where it is most needed.

II

The Brexit Phenomenon

4

Brexit in a
de-globalising world

*"The dogmas of the quiet past are inadequate
to the stormy present."*

Abraham Lincoln

There are myriad views as to why the vote for Brexit happened. Two years on from the outcome of the vote, nobody is clear what Brexit will mean – for Britain, for Europe, or for anyone else.

We have devoted this second section to Brexit because it is an important phenomenon within the context of globalisation that we have described in the first part of this book. Brexit allows us to examine how some of what we have postulated in the first section might apply – or not.

It is not our aim to take an ideological approach to the wisdom or otherwise of Brexit. Rather we aim to interpret Brexit and the environment that exists for post-Brexit trade.

In spite of endless claims and counter-claims, nobody can possibly predict with any degree of certainty the future trajectory of a Britain outside the EU. The world will continue to change in unpredictable ways – as will the UK itself.

Which spectacles?

As always, any event can be looked at through different spectacles. So it is with Brexit.

Brexit as opportunity

There are many ways in which Brexit can be considered an opportunity for Britain.

We have spent quite a bit of time in our first section outlining the strain that international trade places on sovereignty and democratic accountability. We have also described how the European Union has taken the pooling of sovereignty further than most and, with it, the creation of a democratic deficit. At its most basic, Brexit is one manifestation of a broader rebellion against pooled sovereignty and the emasculation of the nation state.

As for trade, in breaking away from the EU with its monolithic harmonisation approach, the UK potentially gives itself more freedom to pursue its self-interest. While negotiating as part of the EU gives the UK added heft (a point we shall come to later), the UK is one voice among many in Europe. European trade agreements have broadly to satisfy many member states all with different priorities.

Negotiating alone, the UK will have more flexibility. It can give way on areas that are less important to its own self-interests (recognition of geographical indications for agricultural products, to give one example) but that could never be negotiated away in a pan-European deal.

Some argue that the need to satisfy so many different interests across Europe is one reason why any trade deal involving the EU ends up being shallow. There is always someone who will object to this or that making anything but the most superficial deals that offend nobody well-nigh impossible.

The need to accommodate many different interests among member states makes EU trade deals necessarily shallow

Freed from harmonised rules and regulations, the UK can also be free to experiment and innovate. Which direction that will take, or even whether it will happen at all, remains to be seen. But the opportunity is there.

To examine these hypotheses further, it is worth looking at the UK's performance in world trade relative to other EU countries in the period since 1972, when the UK joined what was then the Common Market.

As can be seen from the figure below, the UK has performed relatively well in terms of GDP growth during the period. But it has performed much worse than its peers within the EU in the increase in proportion of international trade relative to GDP. Being part of the EU has not prevented others increasing their level of international trade much more successfully than the UK.

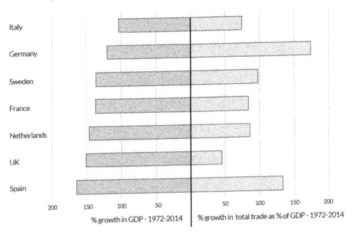

Within the EU, the UK has produced good GDP growth but poor growth in international trade

% growth in GDP - 1972-2014   % growth in total trade as % of GDP - 1972-2014

Source: World Economic Forum

One can come up with different hypotheses for this relatively poor UK trading performance. One is that the UK's de-industrialised economy heavily dominated by services – and in particular financial services – is now poorly placed to be a trading economy. In other words, Global Britain is an illusion.

An alternative hypothesis is that EU rules and trade agreements end up being more aligned with the trading needs of continental economies than with the UK economy, hence limiting the UK's trading opportunities.

No doubt every reader can pick whichever hypothesis happens to confirm their own ideology and pre-conceived ideas.

One more point is worth making. For all the hype about the value, for some the absolute imperative, of international trade, a poor trading performance by the UK over the period has not stopped it outstripping many others in terms of GDP growth.

Localism

We have made much in the previous section of the move towards localism. Brexit could allow Britain to make the most of that opportunity once it is freed from having to accommodate the whole of the EU as 'local'. We have talked about China's "Made in China 2025" plan.

> **The UK should exploit the opportunity to put itself at the forefront of the localism movement**

Something of a similar nature could be used to help British business benefit from the newly found interest in localism. Of course, this is not a substitute for trading internationally but rather a complementary approach that could strengthen the British economy at a time when globalism is under strain.

Brexit as threat

In breaking away from the EU and seeking to negotiate its own wide-ranging trade deals at a time when globalisation is in retreat, Britain could be trying to go against the tide of world affairs. HMS Global Britain might be leaving the safe harbour of the EU and sailing away onto seas that no longer accommodate globalism. The UK might find itself struggling in splendid isolation at a time when everyone else is forming larger negotiating blocs.

The first element in this journey is that Britain is cutting itself loose from one of the world's three large trading blocks in a world that looks to become dominated by competition between these blocks. The UK will reduce the negotiating heft that it had as part of a market of nearly 600 million people. Its voice will matter much less in direct negotiations with China and the US than will the voice of the EU.

> **Is HMS Global Britain leaving safe harbour to sail into inhospitable seas?**

It remains to be seen whether this loss of heft will be compensated, or more than compensated, by the UK's new-found flexibility and reduced bureaucracy;

or whether the result will be that the UK will be at the mercy of the whims and desires of other large trading blocs.

In spite of all sorts of claims and counter-claims delivered with egregious levels of conviction about the shape of a largely unknowable future, the long-term balance of advantages and disadvantages after Brexit are a matter of pure speculation.

What is not so speculative is that, independent of the long-term future, the short-term impact of Brexit will likely be substantially negative.

The UK does nearly £600 billion in trade with the EU; an amount that dwarfs its trade volumes with any other country or bloc (figure).

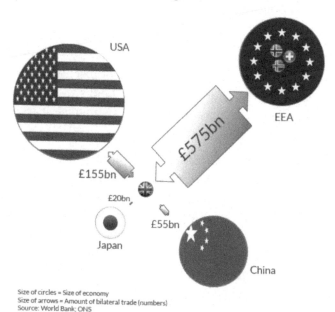

Size of circles = Size of economy
Size of arrows = Amount of bilateral trade (numbers)
Source: World Bank; ONS

It benefits from integrated supply chains and seamless borders. All of that will potentially be disrupted, or at the very least made significantly more difficult, on Day 1 post-exit.

That is why we have previously recommended[42] a five-year transition period where the UK remains part of the EEA/EFTA to allow for longer-term adjustments and for potential trade deals with other countries to be turned into something more concrete than vague assertions and cheerleader performances.

What are the UK's domestic and foreign policy goals post-Brexit?

We have stressed throughout this book that trade is not an end in itself. It is an instrument of domestic and foreign policy. This is an area of discussion that has lacked clarity and cohesion in the Brexit debate – something that, maybe, does not distinguish it from much else in the Brexit debate.

There has been much talk about the desire to strike trade deals with others after Brexit. But what should such trade deals try to achieve and how does that fit with the UK's priorities in domestic and foreign policy? Of course, such priorities will shift as the colour of the UK government changes over time. But have we had any hints of what future trade deals would be expected to deliver?

Maybe the most talked about issue is immigration. The UK wishes to end unlimited immigration from the EU. That is a legitimate policy goal and one that should be achievable. But we have stressed the importance of open cultural exchange and the balance to be struck between controlled immigration and openness to people, skills and ideas.

Next is the idea of sovereignty. We have stressed throughout this book that all trade deals involve a degree of loss of sovereignty. The extent of such loss is not nearly as great with trade agreements as it is with being part of the EU. Nevertheless, loss of sovereignty there will be. How much will depend on the type of agreement and with whom.

For instance, would the UK, who has protested at being subject to the jurisdiction of the CJEU, willingly submit to the jurisdiction of Chinese courts as has been suggested in some deals with China? And will the UK on its own have the negotiating heft to resist such conditions or will it be seen as so desperate to strike trade agreements that other countries will be able to extract demanding terms? There is a hint that some of that is already happening as the UK tries to roll over EU trade agreements with third countries.

The idea that the UK's post-Brexit policy would be to turn itself into a de-regulated tax haven thankfully seem to have been knocked into the long grass – at least for the moment. We have made clear in our earlier analysis that social and environmental externalities are increasingly becoming a factor in trade agreements. A de-regulatory/low tax move by the UK would almost certainly scupper the attractiveness of the UK as a trading partner for most other nations.

> A low regulation, low tax UK would be a most unattractive trading partner for most other nations

It is one thing to have to deal with Jersey or the Cayman Islands, or even Singapore, as tax havens. But the idea that the world's fifth largest economy would set itself up as a tax and regulatory paradise and then expect others to open their markets freely to that economy is a non-starter.

For some, like the current Labour Party, Brexit does allow the pursuit of a domestic policy agenda that would be much more difficult to pursue within the EU. A UK government would have more difficulty with nationalisation, state aid, and a generally more statist approach to the economy if inside the EU rather than outside it. But policy approaches such as state aid will run into opposition with any trade agreement struck with any country. Many of the issues are not EU-specific.

We are not here to comment on the attractiveness or otherwise of the different parties' policy agenda. Merely to draw attention to the fact that it is such an agenda that needs to drive Britain's post-Brexit trade plans not the other way around.

5

Post-Brexit trade deals

"There is no such uncertainty as a sure thing"

Robert Burns

What are the prospects for post-Brexit trade deals within the framework that we are proposing? Here we address five different trade deal targets: the EU, the USA, China, Japan and other countries.

The European Union

Any investment advisor worth his or her salt will always advise that the most important aspect of wealth creation is not to lose any of

> Protecting what you already have is the first principle of wealth creation

your existing wealth. It is much harder to make up for lost wealth than to protect what you have, even at the cost of forgoing the full potential of future growth.

This principle also applies to trade and needs to be borne in mind when negotiating post-Brexit

123

arrangements with the EU. Protecting as much as possible of the UK's trade with the EU must be the UK's priority – at least in the short term.

How much is achievable?

Our main recommendation for future trade arrangements is that they should work to achieve some form of mutual regulatory recognition. This, under all sorts of alternative terms, has essentially become the UK's position in negotiations with the EU.

As a member of the EU, Britain already has full regulatory harmonisation and tariff-free trade with EU and EEA countries. With goodwill on both sides, trade should therefore be able to continue unhindered as long as such regulatory alignment exists. Over time, the UK may wish to depart from some of the EU's regulatory standards – particularly in areas where UK-EU trade is not a priority for either side. This approach has been called 'managed divergence.'

The extent to which such divergence will, in practice, happen is a matter for speculation. It depends on whether one believes in the so-called "Brussels effect' where EU regulations become the effective global standard. *"For all the talk of the EU economic model being in trouble, the 'Brussels effect' is getting stronger,"* according to Anu Bradford, a law professor at Columbia University in New York.[43]

Others disagree and claim there is no objective evidence of such an effect.

Overall, we would support the proposed approach of managed divergence. But what are the chances of it happening?

The obstacle lies in the political framework of the EU – and it may well be insurmountable.

The EU's primary interest is in deepening its own internal market. There is still a long way to go to achieve that. While that process is

The EU prioritises its own internal market over any trade arrangement with third parties

ongoing, the EU has less interest in external than internal trade. If we accept this formulation of the EU's policy priorities, then one can understand why the managed divergence approach is not particularly attractive.

The EU has long experience in travelling in the other direction – managed convergence. This is the process that has been adopted for decades to bring countries into the EU sphere of influence and, eventually, into full membership. The policy goal of trade with other European countries has always been to establish a road to eventual membership – either of the EU or of the EEA/EFTA.

Within this framework, trade agreements with third countries have not been a top priority. Which is another reason why, as we mentioned earlier, EU trade agreements tend to be shallow.

The UK is trying to turn these EU policy priorities on their head. In seeking managed divergence, the UK is asking for a smooth exit from the EU and seeking a much deeper trade relationship with the EU than the EU has ever struck with any other third party. The economic benefits of such an approach for both sides are clear. But the political obstacles are formidable.

Whether this route will be viable or not is almost exclusively in the hands of the EU. There are broadly two choices:

> **The EU-UK negotiations could be seen as an opportunity to define the shape of international commerce for the twenty-first century**

The EU could double down on its traditional policy objective — deepening its own single market and placing trade with third parties well down the list of priorities. As a third country, the UK cannot then expect to be treated any differently from other third countries such as Canada. And it can expect to be treated less well than those third countries (such as Ukraine) for whom the relationship with the EU is seen as an expansion of the EU's sphere of influence and, potentially, a road to membership.

Or the EU could take a different view. It could see UK-EU negotiations as offering the prospect of exploring a new kind of trade deal. One based on the principles we lay out in this book rather than on past thinking. It would allow the EU and the UK to be trailblazers in defining the new kinds of trade relationships fit for our times. It could give both parties the lead in defining the shape of international commerce for the twenty-first century.

It is maybe foolish to try to predict which way this is likely to go. But the odds must be that the UK's departure will not lead the EU to change its priorities or suddenly transform itself from a plodding bureaucracy into a trailblazer in international trade. If anything, it may well increase the bloc's siege mentality and drive whatever approach will minimise the chances of others being tempted down the same route – even if that may not be the most economically advantageous approach – or the approach that most benefits the daily lives of European citizens.

In the end, politics (and short-term politics in particular) will likely trump economics. And EU politics will likely focus on protecting the integrity of the Union itself. Of course, the added complication of the Irish border is a concern for both sides and may end up being the defining factor of any post-Brexit arrangement.

In any bureaucracy, inward focus tends to be a stronger driver than the seeking of new opportunity. However desirable it may be, we are not optimistic that the UK will manage to convince the EU to be bold and innovative and to use the opportunity to be at the cutting edge of future trade relationships.

The USA

In the view of Eurosceptic Right, Brexit is the ticket to a whole world of new trade deals previously deprived by dint of EU membership. The one deal prized more than any other (and talked up the most by the media since June 2016) is one with the United States of America. Both Barack Obama and Hillary Clinton talked of the remoteness of this (the "back of the queue" narrative). Trump has publicly discussed such a deal with the United Kingdom on many occasions. But, given the increasing anti-trade rhetoric and actions from the Trump administration, just how realistic is a US-UK free trade deal? And would any realistic possibility of such a thing have any chance of corresponding to the priorities laid out in the previous chapter?

The US will flex its muscle

The UK is a market around a fifth the size of the American one. The US uses its economic might when it comes to trade agreements – and this is becoming much more the case under the Trump administration than it has been in the past.

It also needs to be borne in mind that the UK currently has a trade surplus with the US (figure). This will not go unnoticed. The US opening stance is likely to be the same as that which US Trade Representative Robert Lighthizer laid out in the opening press conference on the NAFTA renegotiation – that the US wanted assurances that America's trade deficits would not continue. This aligns with our perspective that perpetual unidirectional trade imbalances deficits end up being unsustainable.

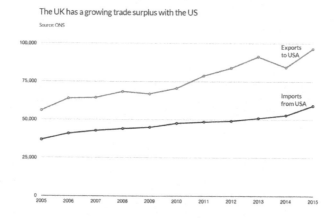

The UK has a growing trade surplus with the US

Source: ONS

For this and other reasons, we do not believe that a comprehensive free trade agreement in the traditional mode will be either easy or particularly successful from the British perspective – at least not during a Trump administration – and possibly not ever.

A new kind of trade deal

Given that, we believe that it may be the possible to strike a new kind of trade deal between the US and the UK along the lines that we have suggested. We believe that the idea of trailblazing a new kind of trade arrangement is aligned with the Trump administration's view that traditional trade agreements no longer serve America's interests.

> **A UK-US trade agreement in the traditional mode seems unlikely**

If the President's rhetoric is true – that he is not anti-trade, but rather against what he sees as deals that are inimical to American interests – then the opportunity to lead the world with a new kind of trade arrangement should be appealing. It could provide a significant political win while creating a template on which the US can start discussions with others on new trade arrangements.

Once again, we see this initially being a platform or framework agreement that can start the process and be continually improved, refined and broadened over time.

Balanced trade over the cycle

Of all our suggestions in the first section, the idea that we should be looking for mechanisms whereby trade balances between countries can be equalised over an economic cycle is the one that would likely be most appealing to the Trump administration. It is, of course, not clear

> **Enshrining the principle of equalising trade balances over the economic cycle could make a US-UK trade deal highly attractive**

how this can be achieved. But enshrining this principle in a new US-UK trade arrangement could significantly enhance the chances of such an agreement being pushed forward and being used as a template for future US trade agreements.

Mutual recognition

There is no reason why this should not appeal to the US administration provided that the sectors selected for discussion are well picked.

There are many sectors, both in goods and services, where standards are similar enough for mutual recognition arrangements to work. The UK and the US also tend to have aligned perspectives in sensitive areas like intellectual property protection. A small selection of appropriate sectors could be a constructive first step towards a trade agreement based on mutual recognition arrangements.

Further, this approach would not require the UK to dilute its regulatory standards thereby avoiding any potential divergence from existing EU standards.

The challenge would be to obtain agreement that some sectors, such as agriculture, would initially be excluded from a trade agreement. This and other sectors have too much divergence in terms of standards, use of subsidies, etc., and are potentially too politically toxic, to allow rapid agreement to be reached.

Our approach of building over time on the basis of a platform agreement is intended to eliminate the need to tackle such sensitive sectors early on, or to allow them to hinder the start of trade in other sectors where agreement can be more easily reached.

Focus on SMEs

This should also appeal to a Trump administration. Trump has positioned his politics as one of defending 'the little guy', the ordinary working American. He has also bumped heads with the CEOs of a number of major corporations on whom he is not as dependent for campaign contributions as other politicians. A US-UK agreement that can be pitched as being in the interests of small business might well have significant political appeal.

Prioritise business and trade over investment

This should also appeal to the Trump administration – although it might face greater hurdles. The prospect of opening markets to the flow of trade in Made in America goods and services would appeal. The challenge could come from abolishing US investor protections, though current NAFTA discussions indicate that the US may well be willing to let these protections go.

Prioritise cultural links, cultural exchange and new thinking

This should also provide a win for both countries provided that one can avoid any perception that it is some kind of back door towards unlimited freedom of movement of people. It should be much easier to limit numbers and circumscribe such an agreement clearly to exclude, for instance, access to social benefits than it has proven possible to achieve between the UK and the EU. Common language and the already existing historical, cultural and research links between the UK and the US and their cultural institutions also form a good basis on which to build further.

Finally, the similarity of the UK and US legal systems should allow for a reasonable dispute resolution mechanism to be constructed.

***

Overall, we believe that our new kind of arrangement is more likely to be successful with the Trump administration than is a traditional all-singing, all-dancing free trade agreement. Of course, the benefits that accrue from this approach will be longer in coming, further emphasising the need for the UK to protect what it already has with the EU. But benefits there will be and with less of the downsides than traditional agreements.

China

The prospects of a similar deal with China are much more dubious. Regulatory standards, attitudes to intellectual property rights, legal systems and cultural expectations are all much more divergent between the UK and China than between the UK and the US.

China is also still at the stage of using foreign direct investment and the power of its major corporations (many state owned or state directed) rather than its smaller companies to project its economic power.

Further, as we have outlined previously, there is no evidence that China has much interest in opening up its market to foreign trade without extracting significant concessions. Such concessions would not be limited to trade but would rapidly spill over *"into overtly political and strategic areas"*[44] such as supporting China policy in the South China Sea and its relations with Taiwan and Tibet.

This use of what has been called China's 'sharp power'[45] has been evident for some time. China punished David Cameron for meeting the Dalai Lama and punished Norway economically for awarding the Nobel Prize to a pro-democracy activist. When a Chinese firm invested in the port of Piraeus, Greece felt it necessary to veto a European statement criticising China's

Trade agreements with China rapidly spill over into demands for political concessions

human rights record. President Duterte of the Philippines promised to 'shut up' about China's illegal occupation of islands in the South China Sea in return for Chinese investment. China intimidated Vietnam into stopping Repsol, a Spanish oil company, from exploratory drilling well inside Vietnamese waters.

The question for the UK government is whether, in the case of China, increased flexibility will make up for significantly reduced economic negotiating heft once it has left the EU. To what extent will the increased flexibility only translate to an ability to abandon some fundamental British political positions and democratic principles? Would the UK be willing to do that in order to secure any form of trade deal with China? The UK government's refusal, so far, to sign up to the Belt and Road initiative and its insistence that the initiative comply with 'international standards'[46] suggests that the UK may not easily bend its political positions to secure a China trade agreement.

Cultural links

There is no doubt potential for increasing cultural links with China. But these come with their own perils.

Australia, New Zealand, Germany, the US and Canada are all starting to raise flags of how Chinese economic, cultural, university and publishing links may be being used to influence national politics.

> *"[China's] sharp power has a series of interlocking components: subversion, bullying and pressure, which combine to promote self-censorship. For China, the ultimate prize is pre-emptive kowtowing by those whom it has not approached, but who nonetheless fear losing funding, access or influence."*[30]

We therefore see little significant near-term prospects of a UK-China trade agreement along the lines we have proposed. And probably not along traditional lines either unless such a deal were overwhelmingly to favour China rather than the UK, and the UK was prepared to abandon long held beliefs and political positions to accommodate China's perspective.

Japan

Japan probably sits somewhere between China and the US in terms of prospects. It is an ally more likely to be open to a level-playing-field type of deal than is China. Regulatory standards in some sectors are more comparable to those in the UK (though they are more stringent in some cases), and intellectual property rights are well protected. Similarly, Japan should be open to strengthening cultural links.

Although, according to the EU, *"Japan continues to be a country where doing business or investing is often challenging due to the features of the Japanese society and economy"[47]*, the recently concluded EU-Japan Economic Partnership Agreement (EPA) and the ongoing discussions about a Strategic Partnership Agreement both offer grounds for optimism.

The EU-Japan EPA has many of the features that we recommend for our platform agreements:

- Mutual recognition in four sectors of the economy and mutual recognition of Authorised Economic Operators.

- Collaboration on anti-competitive action.

- Agreement to collaborate on science and technology.

One should also note the EU's comment that *"The trade relationships between the EU and Japan have usually been characterised by big trade surpluses in favour of Japan."[42]*

Once again, consistent unidirectional trade imbalances are becoming less and less acceptable for deficit countries.

Other countries

What of other countries?

The table below shows which are the next largest group of economies that, *together*, create an economy the same size as that of the EEA/EFTA (excluding Britain). Of these, realistically, only Canada and Australia are likely to be early candidates for the type of trade arrangement that we are proposing.

India	Indonesia
Canada	Mexico
Australia	Turkey
Brazil	Saudi Arabia
Russia	Argentina
South Korea	

Other countries are too far from UK regulatory, legal and cultural standards to make our proposed trade arrangements meaningful. Bespoke arrangements may be possible with some. But how that can be made to fit with maintaining a high degree of access to the EU market remains to be seen.

Roll-over arrangements

Finally, what are the prospects of the UK being able to roll over existing agreements between the EU and third countries once it leaves the Union?

It may be worth dividing this question into two parts: rolling agreements over so that they continue to apply during the Brexit transition period; and rolling them over after the transition period.

The transition period

From a legal point of view, arguments have been made that it should be possible to retain third party agreements during the transition period provided such a provision is included in the Withdrawal Agreement. The "Guernsey Model" has been used to support such a position:

> *"Under the "Guernsey model", the Withdrawal Agreement would provide that the United Kingdom would cease to be a Member State as of (say) 29 March 2019. However, there would be a further provision (the "reservation provision") that would state that, for all purposes connected with the EU's rights and obligations in international law as against third*

countries, the EU Treaties would be regarded as continuing to apply in the United Kingdom until the end of the transitional period."[48]

While one can accept that there are no legal obstacles to such a roll-over, whether it will happen or not depends on the goodwill of the EU and of third countries and the UK's ability to harness any such goodwill. Some countries may see the situation as an opportunity to wring concessions from the UK – as has reportedly already been mooted in the case of South Korea and Chile.[49] Once again, it is persistent trade imbalances that may drive behaviour. South Korea, for instance, has indicated that it would like to address its trade deficit with Britain as part of any agreement.

Post-transition

The question of whether EU-Third Country trade agreements can be rolled over following the transition period has also received much attention. It is beyond the scope of this book to examine the technical details. But it seems likely that *"substantive changes will be necessary when EU trade agreements are rolled over."*[50]

Once again, it is likely that technical issues can be resolved with time. It is the politics of each individual deal and how countries will see the balance of power in negotiations that will determine the outcome.

None of this will be achieved at the stroke of a pen and may be further complicated by differing trade priorities within the

Should the UK look to roll-over existing agreements or to forge a new path?

four nations of the United Kingdom itself.

Yet, would the UK really simply want to roll over existing agreements that are all structured in the traditional mode and intended to satisfy the needs of 28 different countries? Or would it benefit everyone if each deal were converted to the type of platform trade agreement that we are proposing, using the principles we have laid out?

Is this another opportunity to re-think how trade should be structured in the twenty-first century?

III

A globalisation for our times

6

Saving globalisation
from itself

*"The 'anti-globalisation movement' is the
most significant proponent of globalisation
– but in the interests of people, not
concentration of state-private power."*

Noam Chomsky

P rotectionist! Populist!

These are the cries that emanate from some who see themselves as intent on preserving an open trading world whenever anyone suggests that the current international trade system is no longer fit for the economic and geopolitical needs of the twenty-first century. But these are empty words. *"...okay, you've called him a name. You haven't solved anything,"* warns Robert M. Pirsig in *Zen and the Art of Motorcycle Maintenance.*

Some have framed the issue as an ideological battle between a liberal, internationalist camp working to preserve an open, multilateral trading system and an anti-liberal front, led by the Trump administration, intent on closing down free trade. This formulation is quite wrong.

The battle we face is a different one. It is between those who cling to twentieth century thinking based on nineteenth century ideas, refusing to address the shortcomings, in today's world, of the current international trading system and multilateral institutions that underpin it; and those who believe that survival of an open, peaceful world order depends on system reform.

We are in the latter camp. The greatest threat to the multilateral system comes from those who are so invested in its current form (for reasons of personal career, personal profit, or a simple inability to envision alternatives) that they fight to perpetuate an indefensible status quo. Such behaviour is the essential fuel behind the political success of reactionary forces. As such, it is complementary to, and works in tandem with, rather than against, the 'anti-liberal' front. Two seemingly opposing camps actually reinforcing each other politically.

> **Resistance to change is the essential fuel behind the rise of reactionary political forces**

Fortunately, those calling for reform are increasing in number and their voices are getting louder. How one achieves such reform is challenging when faced with entrenched systems and powerful interests intent on maintaining the status quo. President Trump seems to take the view that a robust and uncompromising approach is needed if one is to shake a turgid system out of its stagnation.

Others see such a pugilistic approach as threatening to the stability of the established order. They prefer multi-lateral consultation – in spite of its necessarily glacial pace. Yet others continue to use the rhetoric of defending an open trading system as a mask behind which they aggressively pursue their own self-interest.

For millennia, people have sought to trade with each other. Over time the tools that open up international trade have developed as have the means and technologies that facilitate global commerce. We are strong believers that

> "Globalisation feels like a runaway train. Out of control.
>
> Gordon Brown

people should have both the right and the ability to trade with whomever they wish. The post-war global order made huge strides in opening up global markets. The benefits are clear. As are the accumulating disadvantages in the face of a rapidly changing world.

The time has come to take action to save globalisation from itself. As the geopolitical map changes and globalisation becomes one of the poster children of rising inequality, lack of fairness, dominance by the few, and growing environmental damage, it opens the opportunity for reform.

The applicability of nineteenth century formulations of comparative advantage need re-examination in a world of rapid exchange of information, global movement of skills and capabilities, and a post-industrial economy that shifts and changes almost daily. Their relevance to today's world should, at the very least, be questioned.

These foundations on which the trading system as we know it was built may represent what economists call the time inconsistency of policy – the idea that what was seen as optimal yesterday is no longer optimal today.

Trade is politics

Trade is politics as much as, if not more than, it is economics. It was always so. Cobden's repeal of the corn laws was a fundamentally political act. Free trade as a means of achieving political as well as economic ends.

The eternal challenge is to balance politics and economics

We have argued in this book that trade is an instrument of foreign and domestic policy. It is not an end in itself. What we are seeing today is a structure and flow of trade that, for many countries, is not serving domestic and foreign policy objectives.

It is also naïve in the extreme to believe that one can have cross-border trade without political entanglement. That, in a world where no single country any longer 'rules the waves', one can be a great trading nation without sacrificing some degree of sovereignty.

The challenge lies, as always, in balancing politics and economics. We believe that the framework we have laid out would achieve a better balance than that currently being achieved. It is an attempt to re-focus trade back on to its original propose – that of encouraging innovation and competition rather than featherbedding the already dominant. It puts regulatory alignment front and centre of all trade deals; it focuses primarily on trade as opposed to prioritising investment; it distinguishes between trade and capital flows; it encourages trade deals that benefit MSMEs as well as larger entities; and it emphasizes the importance of cultural links as a way of enhancing mutual understanding and collaboration.

Our approach also recognises the corrosive effects of persistent, unidirectional trade imbalances.

We have tried to bring to the fore the political nature of international trade, the distribution of its wealth creating effects, and the trade-offs that are inevitable between trade and sovereignty.

Multilateral institutions, such as the Bretton Woods Institutions, may well resist our approach. The more political trade is seen to be, the less viable may be the role of institutions that are not seen to have sufficient legitimacy. Multilateral institutions that, today, remain dominated by the West and are not sufficiently accountable to the populations they are supposed to be serving, would need to be reformed significantly if their standing is not to continue to decline.

Brexit is a significant event. Do we interpret it as yet another assertion of the nation state in the face of a globalizing world – and the hyper-integrating type of globalisation epitomised by the European Union? Or do we see it as an article of faith in the future of global trading? How it will all turn out is unpredictable. Yet it could be

> International trade will always have an important role to play in countries' domestic and foreign policy

disruptive enough to offer another opportunity to explore new meanings for 'globalisation' and a substrate on which new types of trade arrangements fit for our times can be built.

We remain optimistic that international trade will always have an important role in countries' domestic and foreign policies. Trade is not there for its own sake. Nor should it be there to deliver highly asymmetric benefits. But, well-structured, with honesty about the advantages and disadvantages of different arrangements, and with a willingness always to adapt to the times and to seek positive change, trade can remain one part of the glue that holds countries and peoples together.

We are not there at the moment. The current trade system risks increasing already rising geopolitical tensions across the globe. A better trading system cannot, on its own, cure such tensions. But it can be part of the armamentarium deployed to encourage harmony and understanding among nations and peoples.

It is worthwhile at this point flicking back and re-reading the quote from J. M. Keynes with which we opened this book. Many today dismiss this statement as a cry for protectionism. It is, of course, nothing of the sort. Keynes was one of the great liberals of his time. But he also had one of the most incisive minds. His words call for balance rather than for extreme, ideologically driven policy. His words are maybe more relevant today than they have ever been.

In this book, we have tried to heed Keynes's advice: *"It should not be a matter of tearing up roots but of slowly training a plant to grow in a different direction."*

References

[1] *Time* (2007), The Best of Asia, 7 May.

[2] Renaud Girard. The diplomatic era of devil-take-the-hindmost. https://radix.org.uk/diplomatic-era-devil-take-hindmost/

[3] Martin Sandbu. The battles of ideology that will define our age. *Financial Times*, December 26, 2017.

[4] Alan Beattie. Bloc's plan is too shallow for it to assume the role of global trade leadership. *Financial Times*, September 26, 2017

[5] Paul Krugman. Is Bilateralism Bad? NBER Working Paper No 2972. Issued May 1989

[6] What the West got wrong. *The Economist*, 3rd March 2018

[7] US should trade carefully on China trade concerns. *Financial Times* editorial. August 6, 2017

[8] Dani Rodrik. The great globalisation lie. *Prospect* Magazine, December 12, 2017.

9 Kai-Fu Lee. China and the UK should be partners in the AI revolution. *Evening Standard.* Wednesday 17 January 2018, p15

10 Fred Hu and Michael Spence. Why Globalisation Stalled. And How to Restart It. *Foreign Affairs*, July/August 2017 Issue

11 Daniel Gros. Whither the Multilateral Trading System? Project Syndicate. December 6, 2017

12 Dani Rodrik. What do trade agreements really do? https://drodrik.scholar.harvard.edu/files/dani-rodrik/files/what_do_trade_agreements_really_do.pdf

13 Dani Rodrik. *The Globalisation Paradox. Democracy and the Future of the World Economy.* WW Norton & Company. March 2012

14 Jean Monnet. *Memoirs.* Doubleday & Company Inc., Garden City, New York. 1978

15 Dani Rodrik. What do trade agreements really do? https://drodrik.scholar.harvard.edu/files/dani-rodrik/files/what_do_trade_agreements_really_do.pdf

[16] Christopher Lakner and Branko Milanovic. Global Income Distribution: From the Fall of the Berlin Wall to the Great Recession. *The World Bank Economic Review* Advance Access published August 12, 2015.

[17] *Making Trade an Engine of Growth for All: The Case for Trade and for Policies to Facilitate Adjustment.* IMF Policy Paper. April 10, 2017.

[18] Adam Corlett. *Examining an Elephant. Globalisation and the lower middle class of the rich world.* Resolution Foundation. September 2016.

[19] Alan Beattie. The flaws of trying to compensate globalisation's losers. *Financial Times*, November 19, 2017.

[20] Caliendo, Lorenzo, and Fernando Parro, "Estimates of the Trade and Welfare Effects of NAFTA," *Review of Economic Studies,* 82, 2015, 1–44.

[21] Hakobyan, Shushanik, and John McLaren, "Looking for Local Labor Market Effects of NAFTA," *Review of Economics and Statistics*, 98(4), October 2016, 728–741.

[22] Paul Krugman. Globalisation: What did we miss? March 2018.

https://www.gc.cuny.edu/CUNY_GC/media/LISCente
r/pkrugman/PK_globalization.pdf

23 Joe Zammit-Lucia. Beyond Governance: Towards a
market economy that works for everyone. Radix Paper
No. 6. 2017. https://radix.org.uk/wp-
content/uploads/2017/02/Beyond_governance_V5_si
ngles.pdf

24 Warwick Lightfoot, Joshua Burke, Nicholas Craig-
Harvey, Jonathan Dupont, Richard Howard, Rebecca
Lowe, Richard Norrie, Michael Taylor. *Farming
Tomorrow: British agriculture after Brexit.* Policy
Exchange, 2017

25 David Pilling. Pilot scheme seeks to produce first
'ethical cobalt' from Congo. Financial Times, March
25th, 2018

26 G20 Leaders' Declaration. Shaping an interconnected
world. Hamburg 7/8 July 2017.
https://www.g20.org/gipfeldokumente/G20-leaders-
declaration.pdf

27 Gillian Tett. Executives take a quiet turn away from
globalisation. *Financial Times.* June 1, 2017

[28] Tim Bradshaw. Self-driving cars raise fears over 'weaponisation.' *Financial Times*. January 14, 2018

[29] Trans-Pacific Partnership Agreement. Chapter 14

[30] The liberalisation and management of capital flows: An institutional view. International Monetary Fund, November 14, 2012

[31] IMF re-opening case for capital controls? The Bretton Woods Project, 5 April 2016. http://www.brettonwoodsproject.org/2016/04/imf-reopening-case-for-capital-controls/

[32] Debate: Should tech firms be taxed on revenue, rather than profit. *City AM*, 26 February 2018.

[33] What the world thinks about globalisation. *The Economist,* November 18 2016.

[34] Robert McDougall. Canada's objectives are similar to Britain's. *Financial Times*. August 25, 2017.

[35] Robert McDougall. Personal Communication. February 2018

36 Graham Allison and Arianna Huffington. Optimizing decision-making in a dangerous world. Project Syndicate. September 4, 2017.

37 Robert McDougall. Personal communication. February 2018

38 Hans Werner Sinn. Europe should not retaliate against American protectionism. Project Syndicate. March 23, 2018.

39 Daniel Kishi. Robert Bork's America. *The American Conservative,* March 1, 2018

40 Peter Foster and Alya Zayed. Whitehall warned it is falling behind in the race to secure post-Brexit free-trade agreements. *Daily Telegraph*, 3 December 2017

41 Natalia T Tamirisa. *Trade in Financial Services and Capital Movements.* International Monetary Fund, July 1999

42 Joe Zammit-Lucia, Nigel Gardner and Nick Tyrone. A Very British Brexit. Radix Paper No 8. June 2017. https://radix.org.uk/wp-content/uploads/2017/06/Brexit_october_report_A5_ePub.pdf

[43] Alan Beattie. Why the whole world feels the Brussels effect. *Financial Times*, November 16, 2017

[44] James Kynge and Michael Peel. Brussels rattled as China reaches out to eastern Europe. *Financial Times*, November 27, 2017

[45] What to do about China's "sharp power". *The Economist*. 14 December 2017

[46] George Parker. Theresa May declines to endorse China's Belt and Road initiative. *Financial Times*. January 29, 2018

[47] http://ec.europa.eu/trade/policy/countries-and-regions/countries/japan/ Accessed 8 March 2018.

[48] George Peretz. How to 'roll over' EU and third country FTAs during the Brexit transition. UK Trade Forum. December 15, 2017.

[49] Hans von der Burchard. EU trade partners demand concessions for Brexit transition rollover. *Politico*. 2 February 2018.

[50] International Trade Committee of the House of Commons. Continuing application of EU trade agreements after Brexit. 6 March 2018

By the same authors...

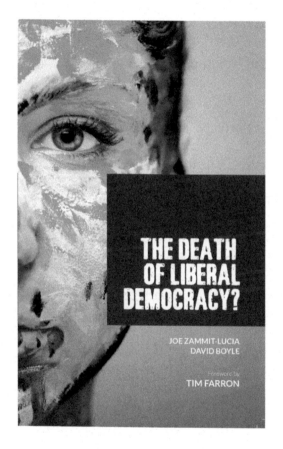

Available on Amazon

Find out more about Radix

The think tank for the radical centre
www.radix.org.uk

Some of the Radix papers available on the web site:

What is the radical centre?

A very British Brexit: A road map

Beyond Governance: An economy that works for everyone

What is the future of trade unionism in Britain?

Working Late: The importance of older women to our economy

Quantitative Easing: The debate that never happened